THE POEMS OF GENERAL GEORGE S. PATTON, JR.

Lines of Fire

We believe that this stirring poem by General Patton will take its place with the world's great war literature. Hitherto unpublished, it was turned over to the Woman's Home Companion recently by Mrs. Patton, who has treasured it ever since her husband wrote it. The general is hailed in the field as "Blood and Guts" Patton, but here he reveals a different side of his character. The wives, mothers and sweethearts of our servicemen will be inspired to learn that one of America's outstanding generals faces the agonies of war with deep solemnity and religious fervor. THE EDITORS

Portrait of
General Patton
by Carolyn Edmundson

God of Battles

by GEORGE S. PATTON, Jr.
Lieutenant General, United States Army

From pride and foolish confidence
From every weakening creed
From the dread fear of fearing
Protect us, Lord, and lead.

Great God, who through the ages
Hast braced the bloodstained hand,
As Saturn, Jove or Woden
Hast led our warrior band,

Again we seek Thy counsel,
But not in cringing guise.
We whine not for Thy mercy—
To slay: God make us wise.

For slaves who shun the issue
We do not ask Thy aid.
To Thee we trust our spirits,
Our bodies unafraid.

From doubt and fearsome 'boding,
Still Thou our spirits guard,
Make strong our souls to conquer,
Give us the victory, Lord.

Lines of Fire

In November 1943, *Woman's Home Companion* published this version of "God of Battles" to show a "different" side of "Blood and Guts" Patton.

Photo courtesy of Perkins Library
Duke University

THE POEMS OF
GENERAL GEORGE S. PATTON, JR.

Lines of Fire

Edited, Annotated and Introduced
by
Carmine A. Prioli

Studies in American Literature
Volume 8

The Edwin Mellen Press
Lewiston/Queenston/Lampeter

Library of Congress Cataloging-in-Publication Data

Patton, George S. (George Smith) 1885-1945.
   [Poems]
   The poems of General George S. Patton, Jr. : lines of fire/
edited, annotated and introduced by Carmine A. Prioli.
    p. cm. -- (Studies in American literature ; vol. 8)
   ISBN 0-88946-162-7
   1. War poetry, American. 2. World War, 1939-1945--Poetry.
I. Prioli, Carmine A. II. Title. III. Series: Studies in American
literature (Lewiston, N. Y.) ; v. 8.
PS3531.A838A6 1990
811'.52--dc20   90-30990
                                                                                                                       CIP

> This is volume 8 in the continuing series
> Studies in American Literature
> Volume 8 ISBN 0-88946-162-7
> SAL Series ISBN 0-88946-166-X

A CIP catalog record for this book
is available from the British Library.

Parts of this book first appeared in the *Journal of American Culture* (8:4 [Winter 1985], 71-81) and *Studies in Popular Culture* (10:1 [1987], 42-50). They are reprinted herein by permission.

Copyright © 1991 Carmine A. Prioli

All rights reserved. For information contact:

The Edwin Mellen Press	The Edwin Mellen Press
Box 450	Box 67
Lewiston, New York	Queenston, Ontario
USA 14092	CANADA L0S 1L0

The Edwin Mellen Press, Ltd.
Lampeter, Dyfed, Wales
UNITED KINGDOM SA48 7DY

Printed in the United States of America

I have a hell of a memory for poetry and war.

—Major George S. Patton, Jr.
to his wife, March 20, 1918.

CONTENTS

List of Illustrations i
Acknowledgments iii
Introduction v
Editorial Note xxiii

I. 1903-1917: West Point and Mexico

A Toast 3
The Five Stages of Cadet Life 4
The Life of a Cadet 6
Beatrice 7
To War 8
The Brave Went Down 11
Servants 12
Oh, Ye Foolish Half-God Mortals 13
Billy the Old Troop Horse 15
Epitaph to a Horse 17
Marching in Mexico 19
Valor 20
The Rulers 22
L'Envoi 25
The Cave Man 28
To Wilson 30
Eternal Peace 32
The Curse of Kant 34
Youth 35
To Beatrice 36
The Fly 38
The Turds of the Scouts 40
The Attack 44
The Vision 46
The Bronco Pass 48

II.   1917-1918: World War I

Mud 53
Dusk 56
The Air Raid 57
The Trench Raid 57
The Song of the Embusqué 58
Rubber Shoes 60
A Code of Action 61
The End of War 62
Memories Roused by a Roman Theater 65
The Precious Babies 68
The Song of the Turds of Langres 69
The Slacker 71
To Your Picture 72
You Never Can Tell About a Woman 73
Recollections – A.E.F. 74
Mercenary's Song (A.D. 1600) 75
Soldier's Religion 77
To Our First Dead 80
Regret 81
The Moon and the Dead 83
Peace – November 11, 1918 84
In Memoriam 87
Bill 88
The Yellow Legs 92

III.   1919-1940: Interlude – Between Wars

The Approach March 99
A Soldier's Burial 100
Dead Pals 101
The Soul of the Guns 103
Ouija 104
Progress 105
Majority Law 107

  Defeat 107
  Florida 108
  Wigglers 109
  The Cays (A Fragment) 111
  The Forgotten Man 111
  The Vanished Race 113
  The Dying Race 113
  Rediscovered 114
  The City of Dreadful Light 115
  The War Horses 116
  Through a Glass, Darkly 118
  Decoration Day 122
  The Lament of the New Heroes 124
  Anti-Climax 124
  Out of Hell 126
  The Soul in Battle 128
  Forgotten Dwellings 129
  The Rape of the Caribbean 130
  The Pacific 131
  The Sword of Lono 133

IV. 1940-1945: World War II
  That Must Be Benson 137
  God of Battles 141
  Seven Up! 143
  Absolute War 146
  The Life and Death of Colonel Gasenoyl 147
  Reference 154
  Oh, Little Town of Houffalize 155
  The Song of the Bayonet 157
  Fear 158
  Duty 161
Bibliography 163
Index 169

ILLUSTRATIONS

Frontispiece. *"God of Battles,"* Woman's Home Companion, 1943.
P. xxiv. Cadet Patton, West Point graduation photo, 1909.
P. 18. 2nd Lt. Patton practicing hurdles for Olympic games, 1912.
P. 27. 2nd Lt. Patton executing mounted saber exercises, 1913.
P. 43. 1st Lt. Patton as aide to Gen. John J. Pershing, 1916.
P. 50. Tanks of Patton's 304th American Tank Brigade, 1918.
P. 67. Lt. Col. Patton and one of his "precious babies," 1918.
P. 79. American War Fund poster, 1918.
P. 91. American tank crew in 6.5-ton "baby" tank, c. 1918.
P. 96. Patton and crew on board the *Arcturus*, 1935.
P. 132. Col. and Mrs. Patton as King Arthur and Guinevere, 1939.
P. 136. "Third Army's Patton," *Time* cover, 1945.
P. 140. Lt. Gen. Patton singing, accompanied by Italian prisoner of war, 1943.
P. 144. Lt. Gen. Mark W. Clark and Lt. Gen. Patton, 1943.
P. 148. Lt. Gen. Patton awarding D.S.C. to Col. "Paddy" Flint, 1943.
P. 153. Lt. Gen. Patton serving victory cake to Col. "Paddy" Flint, 1943.
P. 156. Gen. Patton welcomed home by Mrs. Patton, 1945.
P. 160. Gen. Patton and his decorations, 1945.

ACKNOWLEDGMENTS

I wish to thank General Patton's heirs, Major General George S. Patton and Mrs. James W. Totten, for granting me permission to examine the Patton Papers from 1940-1945 in the Library of Congress. I am especially pleased to acknowledge Mrs. Totten's graciousness and generosity. Her advice often kept me on the right track in pursuing details of her father's poetry that would otherwise have gone unnoticed or unexplained.

I also wish to thank the staffs of the D. H. Hill Library, North Carolina State University; the Davis Library, University of North Carolina at Chapel Hill; the Perkins Library, Duke University; and Fred Bauman of the Library of Congress Reading Room.

David Holt, Librarian at the Davis Memorial Library, Patton Museum of Cavalry and Armor, Ft. Knox, Kentucky, provided invaluable research and photographic assistance.

Gladys T. Calvetti, Rare Book Curator at the U. S. Military Academy Library, West Point, provided several important insights into Patton's early military career. Also at West Point, Colonel Roger H. Nye was generous with both his time and advice on Patton's reading, and Cadet James Keating enlightened me on the General's continuing influence on future Regular Army officers.

I am grateful to Martin Blumenson for his early encouragement and expert judgment. My debt to his meticulous work with the Patton Papers is evident throughout this book.

Georgiana Baker, Richard Baker, Mary Wallace and Robert Wallace provided useful leads on Patton's literary allusions. Professor Edward Linenthal of the University of Wisconsin reviewed the manuscript and offered an array of intelligent and sensitive comments.

For their tactful criticisms and support, I am indebted to my friends, the Reverend Joseph Mann, Susan Edgerton, Porter Williams and Stuart Buck; to my colleagues at North Carolina State University, Antony Harrison, Sanford Kessler, Allen Stein and, especially, to Deborah Wyrick for her generous and insightful comments.

At North Carolina State University I also owe thanks to the Research Committee of the College of Humanities and Social Sciences for travel funds; to the English Department and its Chair, John Bassett, for research time; and to Charlene Turner, Veronica Norris and Carol Sharpe of the English Department secretarial staff for their patience and assistance.

I am greatful for the efforts of the staff of Mellen Book Design who labored long and creatively with introductions, text and footnotes.

My greatest debt is to my wife, Elizabeth, and my son, John, for their love and endurance.

C. A. P.
Chapel Hill, North Carolina

INTRODUCTION

Next to war, poetry was one of the great passions of George S. Patton, Jr. According to his daughter, Ruth Ellen Patton Totten, the "Old Man" had a poem for every occasion, a quote for all the ills and foibles of mankind. Once, Mrs. Totten recently recalled, when she was considering postponing something, the General said to her:

> I dreamed to wait my pleasure,
>   unchanged my spring would bide
> Therefore, to wait my pleasure,
>   I put my spring aside
> Till first, in face of fortune,
>   and last, in 'mazed disdain
> I made Diego Valdez High Admiral of Spain.

"We would always look up the source of his quotes," Mrs. Totten remembered, "and I guess, in that way, we learned a lot of poetry and philosophy too."[1]

So, poetry was not just an incidental pastime for the Patton family. It was one aspect of a literary consciousness initiated by the General's own father, also George S. Patton, who entertained and instructed his children and grandchildren by reciting the *Iliad* to them. Reading from the original Greek, he translated into English as he went along. A graduate of the Virginia Military Institute and a successful lawyer and businessman, the elder

---

1. Letter, Ruth Ellen Patton Totten to Carmine A. Prioli, September 4, 1988. The lines of poetry are from "The Song of Diego Valdez" by Kipling. *Rudyard Kipling's Verse: Definitive Edition* (New York: Doubleday, Doran, 1945), pp. 152-55.

Patton was an avid student of literature who cultivated an appreciation for letters in his son, in part, by catering to the younger Patton's early and voracious appetite for the exploits of ancient warriors and medieval knights. Then followed his son's eager recitations, backyard performances, and, later, literary efforts of his own.

The millions of Americans who either served under General Patton or who know him through films and biographies realize that he wrote poetry of some kind, but few are aware of the extent of his literary output. In fact, Patton could spin out a satirical poem or song in minutes. He could think almost as easily in rhyme and meter as in prose, because much of the popular poetry of the nineteenth and early twentieth centuries was second nature to him. Among poets, Kipling appears to have been his favorite and chief model, but *The Home Book of Verse* was the General's poetic landscape and his taste ran from Homer and Shakespeare to Scott, Macaulay, Tennyson, Longfellow and the "Canadian Kipling," Robert W. Service. From their plundered forms and meters he constructed many of his own verses.

Popular music, too, supplied Patton with language and rhythms that he tried with limited success to imitate. Musically knowledgeable readers may recognize traces of religious hymns, Gilbert and Sullivan, and others in some of the General's verses and songs. One example of the General's adaptation of a well-known melody can be seen in his "Oh, Little Town of Houffalize" (p. 155), a World War II take-off on Phillips Brooks' "O, Little Town of Bethlehem":

> Oh little town of Houffalize,
> How still we see thee lie;
> Above thy steep and battered streets
> The aeroplanes sail by.
>
> Yet in thy dark streets shineth
> Not any goddamned light;
> The hopes and fears of all thy years,
> Were blown to hell last night. [2]

---

2. The relevant lines of "O, Little Town of Bethlehem" are:
> O little town of Bethlehem
> How still we see thee lie!
> Above thy deep and dreamless sleep
> The silent stars go by;

vii

In similar fashion, Patton appropriated the melody and chorus of Stephen Foster's "Nelly Was a Lady" and wrote his satiric poem, "Seven Up!" (p. 143). The chorus of Foster's song, a favorite of barber-shop quartets, is:

                Yet in thy dark streets shineth
                The ever-lasting Light;
                The hopes and fears of all the years
                Are met in thee tonight.
Song and Service Book for Ship and Field: Army and Navy (New York: A. S. Barnes, 1942), p. 83.

    3. *A Treasury of Stephen Foster* (New York: Random House, 1946), pp. 55-57.

The first stanza of "Seven Up!" is:

> Once there was an Army
> Then one day it died
> So toll the bell and waken Hell
> To give it room inside.

Patton was surely not a great poet, as anyone who skims through this volume will quickly see. But his revisions indicate that he often was a serious one, experimenting with forms such as the lyric, ballad, elegy and mock epic. While acknowledging the inadequacies of his "so-called poems" and his own limitations, Patton often revised for clarity and directness, striving to articulate what he termed his "prevailing idea." At one time – between wars – the General assembled a collection of manuscripts that he intended to publish anonymously. He failed at this because his poetical skills fell far short of his military genius.

Delivered with oratorical gusto or tongue-in-cheek wit, poetry was Patton's vehicle for venting the overflow of his energetic personality. It was also his means for establishing comradeship with rhymed profanity and coarse, barracks- and stable-bred humor. "Vulgar and smutty" were the adjectives Patton's father used in 1919 to describe one of his son's poems, probably "The Song of the Turds of Langres" (p. 69). But poetry was also an outlet for artistic expression, for immortalizing the General's innermost thoughts, and for memorializing the sacrifices of heroic men. And poetry was Patton's tonic, keeping him more or less on balance when he was deeply hurt or depressed. After being severely reprimanded by Eisenhower for making some indiscreet public comments in 1944 (comments that nearly cost him command of the Third Army), Patton noted in his diary that he felt like he had "just been killed" and then added: "All the way home, five hours, I recited poetry to myself."[4]

What poems did the General toll out during those dejected hours? Apart from a few lines from Kipling, he left no indication, but his power of recall was nearly total, enabling him to draw upon the vast storehouse of classical and popular literature he had absorbed since early childhood, even

---

4. "Diary," May 1, 1944, Patton Papers, Box 4, Library of Congress, Washington, D.C.

before he became infatuated with the "Mistress War."[5] And, of course, he had his own substantial body of poems, written over a lifetime of military service.

* * * *

Early in 1945, while George Patton was training the guns of the American Third Army on Hitler's Reich, Mrs. Beatrice Ayer Patton submitted one of her husband's poems for publication in *Collier's* magazine. Although it was composed by modern America's most flamboyant and controversial general, the poem was promptly returned because the editors were disinclined to publish anything that would revive the "Old Blood and Guts legend." Moreover, the rejection letter politely explained, this poem–entitled "The Song of the Bayonet" (p. 157)–would probably be regarded as "the song of General Patton."[6]

"From the hot furnace, throbbing with passion," declares the bayonet, "First was I stamped in the form to destroy." In succeeding lines the personified weapon intones its frustration at being used only in mock combat against straw men until, one morning "wet and o'erclouded," its "long thirst" is quenched by the bloodshed of actual battle.

The *Collier's* editors were probably right about their readers' likely response. Since the end of the European conflict was in sight, peace-conscious Americans were becoming increasingly uncomfortable with Patton's aggressiveness. Moreover, the bayonet's savage crooning would

---

5. Throughout the campaigns of 1944 and 1945, Patton carried with him a Bible, the Book of Common Prayer, Caesar's *Commentaries* and, according to Mrs. Patton, "a complete set of Kipling." Beatrice Ayer Patton, "A Soldier's Reading", *Armor: The Magazine of Mobile Warfare,* 61:6 (November-December 1952): 10-11.

6. The letter to Mrs. Patton (March 16, 1945) and her typescript of "The Song of the Bayonet" are included in the George S. Patton Papers, Box 60, Library of Congress. The nickname "Blood and Guts" was coined by Patton in 1936 to describe what he thought was an essential quality for the commandant of cadets at West Point. Later, the sobriquet was applied to Patton–with his blessing–by newspaper reporters. Martin Blumenson, *The Patton Papers: 1885-1940,* vol. I (Boston: Houghton Mifflin, 1972), p. 911; Ladislas Farago, *Patton: Ordeal and Triumph* (New York: Ivan Obolensky, 1963), pp. 142-44.

In spite of the editor's rejection of "The Song of the Bayonet," *Collier's* had run a full-length article on Patton, January 13, 1945.

surely have played into the hands of the General's severest critics, who regularly assailed him as a vulgar and egotistical maniac. But *was* "The Song of the Bayonet" the song of George S. Patton, Jr.? The General's most distinguished biographer, Martin Blumenson, and others have declared that Patton's violent and tough characteristics were "fundamentally alien" to him, that his "inner reality" contrasted with the caricature, the "exaggerated version of what he aspired to be." In the process of developing the outward persona of the ruthless, at times raging warrior, Patton almost killed "the gentle soul within himself."[7] Lieutenant Colonel Charles Codman, the General's aide during World War II, recounted that the "one unresolved problem" in understanding Patton's character was "the reconciliation of the fighting soldier and the gentle man."[8]

Did such a "reconciliation" exist in Patton's life? Was there ever a period when the soldier coexisted with the gentle man? Surely, there were not many times when the latter personality was apparent to the world since – as the General was keenly aware – gentleness and accompanying attributes like compassion and sensitivity do not fire up the killer instinct. His emotional visits to World War II army field hospitals were notable exceptions, but even these expressions of gusty tenderness were, according to Codman, "quick switches" calculated to impress hospital staff personnel.[9] And, of course, the memory of these visits was stained in the popular mind by the notorious "slapping" incidents.[10]

Since Patton's gentleness was by and large not a quality of his public persona, one might reasonably expect to find it illustrated in his private papers, especially in the scores of poems he wrote during forty years of military service. Indeed, some of these poems do reveal gentleness, at least as the term is conventionally understood: sympathy for the suffering of

---

7. Martin Blumenson, *The Patton Papers: 1940-1945*, vol. II (Boston: Houghton Mifflin, 1975), p. 843.

8. Charles R. Codman, *Drive* (Boston: Little, Brown, 1957), p. 275.

9. Codman, p. 111.

10. See introduction to "Seven Up!" p. 143.

animals,[11] particularly horses; empathy with the loves and terrors of the common foot soldier; devotion to his wife; appreciation for the beauty of nature; and, in the words of one biographer, an "inner yearning for a beauty which has nothing to do with 'blood and guts.'"[12]

But Patton's belligerent nature was never mellowed or tempered by his esthetic sense, and poems illustrating "gentle" themes comprise only a small fraction of the total. Most of the General's verses have *everything* to do with blood and guts because, like the epic poetry of ancient times, they reveal a moral attunement to war's ugly brutality and its terrible grandeur. They are also products of an essentially nineteenth-century attitude that accepted war as the universal condition of mankind.

In varying degrees, this was the view of men who deeply influenced Patton's character and, in some cases, helped advance his career. Henry L. Stimson and Leonard Wood are but two examples. As a young cavalry officer stationed at Ft. Myer, Virginia, in 1912, Patton began his lifelong friendship with Stimson, a fellow horseman and Secretary of War under Presidents Taft and Franklin D. Roosevelt. A vigorous sportsman and soldier who wrote and lectured enthusiastically about the "joy of war,"[13] Stimson took a personal interest in Patton, an interest that endured three decades of peace, war and personal controversy. At the same time, Patton rode with and served as aide to Army Chief of Staff, General Leonard Wood, the former Indian fighter and commander of the Rough Riders. General Wood was a tireless proponent of military preparedness and was motivated by the belief that the survival of the fittest was "the general law which

---

11. A school composition that Patton wrote in 1902 illustrates his early sensitivity to the world around him and, for a seventeen-year old, an unusually perceptive view of life in general. It also helps balance the lavender sentimentality that had a tendency to creep into his poetry:

A peculiarly touching little incident of bird life occurred to a caged female canary. Though unmated, it laid some eggs, and the happy bird was so carried away by her feelings that she would offer food to the eggs, and chatter and twitter, trying as it seemed, to encourage them to eat! The incident is hardly tragic, neither is it comic. (Blumenson, I, p. 41.)

12. James Wellard, *General George S. Patton, Jr.: Man Under Mars* (New York: Dodd, Mead, 1946), p. 14.

13. N. Current, *Secretary Stimson: A Study in Statecraft* (New Brunswick, N.J.: Rutgers University Press, 1954), p. 26.

governs all things."[14] Both Stimson and Wood were strapping exponents of the "strenuous" life and the manly virtues it engendered, and they were close friends of Theodore Roosevelt, the man who defined that lifestyle for his generation.

But Patton's poems – especially early ones like "To War," "Valor" and "The Cave Man" (pp. 8, 20 and 28) – illustrate that his conception of manhood and his zest for fighting outmatched even the virile frontier romanticism of Roosevelt and his disciples. Patton's brand of machismo was a patchwork of Nordic mythology and medieval chivalry extracted, in large measure, from the superman philosophy of Thomas Carlyle; social Darwinism and the white man's burden; American nationalism and the vehement ideology of Prussian military theorists. One of these, German Marshal Helmuth von Moltke, attached divine significance to war and believed that continued strife was essential to the health of civilization.[15] Another, General Friedrich von Bernhardi, spoke of war as "not only a biological necessity, but...a moral necessity" indispensible to man because without it "there could neither be racial nor cultural progress."[16]

Patton did not agree with all of Bernhardi's precepts, but he accepted these and at least two others: "That it being impossible to surpass the enemy in every detail, it is consequently necessary to select some one detail which you consider of paramount importance and vastly excell him in that." Since Patton believed that Bernhardi's principle applied to individuals as well as to nations, he advised his father to follow it during his unsuccessful 1915

---

14. Quoted in Richard Hofstadter, *Social Darwinism in American Thought* (rev. ed., New York: George Braziller, 1969), p. 191.

15. Hofstadter, p. 172.

16. Friedrich von Bernhardi, *Britain as Germany's Vassal* [original title, *Our Future – A Word of Warning to the German Nation* (1912)], J. Ellis Barker, trans. (London: 1914), pp. 111, 114. Bernhardi's influence was also apparent later when Patton was developing his philosophy of aggressive fighting. His copy of Bernhardi's *The War of the Future* (1921) on deposit in the U. S. Military Academy Library is heavily annotated. Patton seemed especially impressed with the chapter on "Attack, Defence and Initiative," which expressed Bernhardi's preference for offensive rather than defensive warfare.

campaign for the U. S. Senate.[17] In addition, Patton agreed with Bernhardi that wars are ennobling because they "give scope to strength, greatness and truth, to all the virtues, to unselfishness and to the joy of sacrifice."[18] Shortly after his first combat engagement in World War I, Patton recalled: "War is the only place where a man really lives."[19] Later, as a three-star general, he proclaimed to thousands of American soldiers that "Battle is the most magnificent competition in which a human being can indulge." He added: "It brings out all that is best; it removes all that is base."[20]

It is not surprising, therefore, that the majority of General Patton's poems are far from gentle, because they often recount intensely personal wars. Some are peppered with profanity. A few are blatantly scatological and others, intended to blast pacifist sensibilities, glorify war as the foundation and mainstay of modern civilization. With a handful of exceptions, the poems are technically unsophisticated and often overreach themselves. The thinking behind them is single-minded and predictable. The milder ones are sentimental beyond rescue. Even the more polished ones are often freighted with some excruciatingly bad lines, with meter that refuses to scan, with rhymes that fall flat or clatter like tanks. Although Patton saw a few of his poems achieve some wartime popularity, there is little evidence indicating that even *he* was entirely satisfied with the results of his literary forays.

So why publish them? Why read them?

Because any documents that shed light on the character of one of America's towering folk heroes are inherently valuable, especially if they were written by the man himself. In 1920 Patton confessed half-ironically to a friend that his poems "give a better index to my utter depravity than anything else that I know of."[21] Indeed, the General's poems highlight

---

17. Letter to "Papa," March 9, 1915, Patton Papers, Box 7, Library of Congress. See also Patton's letter to his father on May 16, 1915, in which he says that limiting the rules of war to established precedents would "preclude progress." Blumenson, I, p. 289.

18. Bernhardi, *Britain as Germany's Vassal*, p. 116.

19. Blumenson, I, p. 700.

20. Blumenson, II, p. 269. Also, pp. 398, 421, 718.

21. Fred Ayer, Jr., *Before the Colors Fade* (Boston: Houghton Mifflin, 1964), p. 67.

aspects of his life and personality often hidden from public scrutiny. They help us penetrate the "mask" of command and unfold the private character of a leader upon whose shoulders rested the stars of generalship and the fates of many thousands of human beings, military and civilian.

Because they are not all bad. A few, especially satirical ones like "Recollections – A.E.F." and "Seven Up!" (pp. 74 and 143), must have been uproariously effective when bawled out in person by the General, and they demonstrate a sense of humor about himself rarely exhibited by leaders of his stature. While everyone who personally knew Patton thought of him as a "consummate actor," thousands of American soldiers almost routinely witnessed him upstaging even seasoned professionals. His aide remembered that theater people seemed to have "a lingering effect on the General, that of inciting him – quite unconsciously – to outperform them. As host to galaxies of stars at Palermo, he consistently topped Bob Hope and successively reduced Jack Benny and Al Jolson to straight-men roles."[22]

Because they *do* show that Patton had a "soft" side and was capable of gentleness and deep "poetic" feeling, even if they fail to illustrate these qualities as much as some of the General's biographers would like. Moreover, the poems indicate, first, that Patton was a man whose grasp of military history and theory was complemented by an appreciation for imaginative literature (however limited in scope) far superior to that of his peers and most of the civilian population. Second, they reveal that he augmented his knowledge of literature with the *practice* of it. He not only wrote poetry, but also tried his hand at several short stories and, during World War II, had contemplated writing a novel. Third, they indicate that Patton was a soldier writing and speaking principally for other soldiers, not a poet laboring purely for the sake of art or critical acclaim.

And on at least one occasion, Patton's men wrote poetry for him. Shortly before the invasion of Sicily in 1943, the General sent his wife some verses composed by two soldiers "of tent 21." He characterized the poems as "terrible," but added "the spirit is right."[23] The General meant no put-down,

---

22. Codman, p. 182. Also Farago, pp. 637-38.

23. Letter to "Darling B," June 9, 1943, Patton Papers, Box 13, Library of Congress.

for he could just as easily have been describing his own poetry – "terrible...but the spirit is right."

Perhaps, too, the Patton poems should be read because they challenge the preconception that the professions of arms and of poetry are antithetical. Patton certainly admitted to no such dichotomy, nor did he fear that public knowledge of his poetry would "soften" his warrior image. Even during the tumultuous days of World War II, popular home front magazines (*Collier's* rejection of "The Song of the Bayonet" notwithstanding) were clamoring for anything from his pen. With her husband's knowledge, Mrs. Patton approved for publication several of Patton's poems, including "A Soldier's Burial," "God of Battles" and "Fear" (pp. 100, 141 and 158).

On the war front, Patton's reputation as a poet was widely publicized over the airwaves on December 12, 1943, when the American Expeditionary Radio Station in Palermo broadcast a "Musical Review" dedicated to the General. The program was remarkable for its combination of musical talent, both American and Sicilian. It began with "The 2nd Armored Division March" (composed by Mrs. Patton in 1941) and continued with "The Force of Destiny," a tenor and baritone duet, Franz Liszt's *Liebesträume*, a violin solo, and other selections. The evening's program culminated in Patton's own "God of Battles," set to music by a Captain Rubinstein, orchestrated and played "by the Italian prisoners of war." The piece was sung by "The Port Headquarters Octet."[24]

Finally, General Patton's poems should be read because they reveal, at least as sharply as does his prolific and colorful prose, the essential elements of his character. They provide avenues toward understanding his personality that other written sources, including his published letters and diaries, do not. For example, rarely in his voluminous prose writings does he talk about his belief in reincarnation. But in poems like "Memories Roused by a Roman Theater," "Ouija," "Through a Glass, Darkly" and others (pp. 65, 104 and 118), this belief is developed fully. Patton knew Aristotle's idea about poetry's capacity to express the "universal" truths of human existence,

---

24. In 1947 a copy of the program was sent to Mrs. Patton by its producer, Lieutenant Colonel Harold E. Hopping. It is now in Box 34, Patton Papers, Library of Congress.

while history and, therefore, prose writing tend to express the particular. So there must have been something about the medium of poetry that allowed Patton to explore certain mystical themes, themes that were apparently not suited to the more mundane vehicles of the military journals and lecture podiums.

Other aspects of his character as revealed in the General's poetry are unpleasant. Although he was one of America's most outspoken patriots, he harbored principles deeply at odds with basic democratic ideals: Sparta, not Athens was Patton's ideological home. A devout, Bible-reading Episcopalian, the General also had a pantheon in his head: Saturn, Jove and Woden – not Christ – were the gods he invoked in a prayer to brace "the bloodstained hand." (See "God of Battles," p. 141.) Valhalla, not heaven, was his objective. *Arété*, the classical "combination of proud and courtly morality and warlike valour,"[25] not *détente*, was his battle cry. Discipline, total devotion to duty, adoration of war and the fighting spirit, uncontained hatred for what Patton called "fecal Pacifists," these were his stimulants; these were the ideals he extolled with unabashed frankness in his poetry.

Without question, Patton's military talents and training, his instinct for making the decisive move at the right moment, led to his spectacular World War II successes. But his wartime triumphs were also due to his nearly mythical public character: a gun-toting demi-god able to galvanize and entertain thousands of American troops, while simultaneously unfettering his "bayonet psychology" (see p. 157) to menace the confidence of their enemies. Whether American soldiers took Patton's tough-guy image seriously is highly questionable. It was no secret even to the General that his men most often referred to him as "Georgie." But their German and Italian counterparts, having already empedestalled their own grandstanding demi-gods in Rome and Berlin, took Patton very seriously. During the war, it was the General's barber, a Sicilian by birth, who confirmed for Patton what he already

---

25. Werner Jaeger, *Paideia: The Ideals of Greek Culture,* Gilbert Highet, trans., 3 vols. (New York: Oxford University Press, 1943-1945), I, p. 5. See Also Edward Tabor Linenthal, *Changing Images of the Warrior Hero in America: A History of Popular Symbolism* (New York and Toronto: The Edwin Mellen Press, 1976), chap. 1, "The Chevalier in America: Washington, Custer and Patton."

believed about certain European temperaments. In his diary, the General recorded the comments of a "Corporal Matassa" who advised Patton not to deal too gently with his former countrymen. They are "used to, and need," he said, "an iron hand."[26]

Even Hitler came to recognize in Patton "the gravest and most immediate threat,"[27] while the Führer's subordinates respected Patton as "the adversary they most feared in battle."[28]

Clearly, it was the psychological force of his public character that made Patton such a formidable leader. As one of his junior officers said, Patton was "ninety percent psychology – and ten percent killing!"[29] He had models, of course: Caesar and Hannibal, Alexander and Bonaparte. But he also accepted Aristotle (who was Alexander's tutor) and his pronouncements that poetry was power, that the silver-tongued orator could engage the passions and thus change the course of human destiny. Patton knew that such power moved Plato to ban poets from his "well-ordered state." The ancient Greeks called this power *psychagogia*, the force of art to lead the souls of men.[30] The General did not use exactly that term, but he surely practiced it, excelled in it by forging a public figure unique in modern American history. As a soldier, he was a man of primeval sensibilities; as a poet he was outspoken and shocking, hilarious and maudlin, and at least as brazen as he was publicly on the commander's dais.

* * * *

---

26. "Diary," December 2, 1943, Patton Papers, Box 3, Library of Congress.

27. Farago, p. 592; also, 400, 407, and 505-506. See also George Creel, "Patton at the Payoff," *Collier's*, January 13, 1945, p. 25; Robert Leckie, *Delivered from Evil: The Saga of World War II* (New York: Harper & Row, 1987). Leckie contends that Hitler saw Patton as the Allies' "best general," whose reputation helped to induce Hitler to issue "perhaps his most stupid order of the war" (p. 748).

28. Blumenson, I, p. 4; II, p. 654. See also Blumenson's *Patton: The Man Behind the Legend, 1885-1945* (New York: William Morrow, 1985), p. 296. Further evidence of German regard for Patton over other American army commanders is that he is "the only one to be mentioned *by name* in the postwar accounts and memoirs of the leading German generals." See Charles Whiting, *Patton's Last Battle* (New York: Stein & Day, 1987), p. 188.

29. Quoted in Whiting, p. 41.

30. Jaeger, I, pp. 36, 248.

When T. S. Eliot edited the poems of Rudyard Kipling, he wrote that "part of the fascination of this subject is in the exploration of a mind so different from one's own."[31] Many readers of Patton's verses will agree that they reveal a mind "different" from theirs. War and mankind's warring spirit are not things most people think about in peacetime, so many of Patton's poems will blister, perhaps burn most non-military sensibilities. But as radical as the General's thinking and character surely were, he embodied the aspirations of many thousands of World War II and Vietnam-era Americans.

During the Korean conflict the army honored the General when it named its new M-46 tank after him. For the next decade the "Patton" became the mainstay of the U. S. armored force and today comprises a majority of the army's Reserve and National Guard tank fleets.

The Patton Museum of Cavalry and Armor at Fort Knox is one of the U. S. Army's largest and most popular attractions. Visitors have increased steadily since its founding in 1948, and exceeded 350,000 in 1988. Also in 1988, a second museum, privately sponsored in association with the U. S. Bureau of Land Management, was established on the site of Patton's World War II Desert Training Center, Chiriaco Summit, California.

Since Patton's death in 1945, popular interest in his life has never abated. He has been the subject of two novels, about two dozen book-length biographies (half of which are for "adolescent" readers), four documentaries (narrated by Walter Cronkite, Mike Wallace, Ronald Reagan and Hal Holbrook) and two feature films.

The most stunning and arguably the most memorable expression of American patriotism to come out of the early 1970s was the giant flag that formed the backdrop for the opening speech in *Patton*, the movie. More than twenty years after Francis Ford Coppola wrote the film's screenplay, a contemporary critic has observed that *Patton* "brought two halves of a split society together in movie theatres to marvel at the relevance of a World War

---

31. T. S. Eliot, ed., *A Choice of Kipling's Verse* (1941; rpt., London: Faber and Faber, 1976), p. 17.

II general to the turmoil of the Vietnam era."[32] In 1971 the film was nominated for ten Oscars and won seven, including "Best Picture" and "Best Director," while the award for "Best Actor" went to George C. Scott for his performance as General Patton.[33]

Richard Nixon's decision to invade Cambodia in 1970 was made after he had repeatedly watched *Patton*, the movie.[34] Later, Nixon closely identified with the celluloid version of the beleaguered General when the President was trying to hang tough in the tumultuous, waning days of his administration.

Commemorative postage stamps honoring Patton have been issued by the United States (1), Luxembourg (4), and Belgium (5). In France hundreds of communities have streets and squares named for him.

Although elements of Patton's style appeared anachronistic even in the 1940s, the attitude he struck and the persona he created still engage mainstream imaginations. As late as 1974, he was described in *Newsweek* as "probably the last heroic gasp in the proud myth of American invincibility."[35] He cut a dazzling figure, half-comic but foursquare and profane. In an era when the symbol of the American hero had lost its force, indeed, even its

---

32. Jeffrey Chown, *Hollywood Auteur: Francis Coppola* (New York: Praeger, 1988), p. 1. Chown also notes that Coppola was paid $50,000 in 1966 to write the *Patton* screenplay (p. 23) and as controversy about the Vietnam war began to mount, "he consciously attempted to adopt a position toward the main character that would appeal to doves and hawks alike, more concerned with his own success than with his personal opinion about war" (p. 122).

33. Objecting to the competitive nature of the awards process, Scott refused to accept his Oscar, and it has therefore never been officially issued. Frank McCarthy, the producer of *Patton*, donated the "Best Picture" Oscar to the Virginia Military Institute, where in 1903-1904 Patton spent a year as a cadet. Patton's father and grandfather were graduates of VMI.

In addition to the awards for Best Picture, Best Acting and Best Directing, *Patton* also won Oscars for Story and Screenplay, Art Direction-Set Direction, Sound and Film Editing. The film was nominated for Cinematography (losing to *Ryan's Daughter*), Music (losing to *Love Story*), and Special Visual Effects (losing to *Tora! Tora! Tora!*). Richard Shale, *Academy Awards: An Ungar Reference Index* (New York: Ungar, 1978), pp. 505-508.

34. Rowland Evans, Jr. and Robert D. Novak, *Nixon in the White House: The Frustration of Power* (New York: Random House, 1971), pp. 252, 278. See also Hugh Sidey, "The Presidency: 'Anybody see *Patton*?'" *Life*, June 19, 1970, p. 2B.

35. S. K. Overbeck, "Total Warrior" [review of Blumenson's *The Patton Papers: 1940-1945*], *Newsweek*, October 7, 1974, p. 98.

legitimacy, Patton was an invigorating reminder of a time when men and machines could still be mastered, a time when Americans had never lost a war or had to acknowledge that the blood of their servicemen and women had been shed in vain.

Near the end of World War II, Gerald W. Johnson surely overstated the effect of Patton's post-war influence when he predicted that the General's triumphs would wither the condescension of foreign intellectuals toward American culture, would, in fact, make them notice that "Whitman was a poet, Jefferson a statesman, [and] Emerson a philosopher." It was no exaggeration, however, to say that Patton represented—for better and for worse—a distinctly New World prizefighter's ethos. To Johnson and to millions of Americans who could not articulate the idea so succinctly, "Prometheus Patton" was "the incarnation and glorification, the archetype and the apotheosis of a bust in the snoot."[36]

Today, Patton and his speeches are quoted by management consultants and sales training experts as shining models of the aggressive spirit.[37] A popular college writing handbook cites Patton as a master of rhetoric, along with Patrick Henry, Franklin Delano Roosevelt and Martin Luther King, Jr.[38]

Modern warfare seems increasingly to demand that military officers be trained more as business managers than combat commanders. Resistance to this trend is perhaps why Patton is idolized by the present generation of West Point cadets, most of whom have not yet developed a taste for the starkly unchivalric, impersonal age of technocratic warfare. Naturally, it is at West Point where the Patton legend lives on most warmly and where it

---

36. Gerald W. Johnson, "Prometheus Patton," *Virginia Quarterly Review*, 21:2 (Spring 1945): 274, 277.

37. See, for example, Porter B. Williamson, *Patton's Principles* (Management/Systems Consultants, 1979), esp. chaps. "Principles of Command and Management," "Principles for Making Decisions" and "Principles for Success." Since its publication, Williamson's book is reported to have sold 100,000 copies.

38. James A. Heffernan and John E. Lincoln, *Writing: A College Handbook*, 3rd ed. (New York and London: Norton, 1990), p. 7.

continues to be sustained. In the words of Colonel Robert A. Turner, West Point's Director of Military Instruction, "General Patton is...one of our prime sources of cadet role models."[39]

Whatever the reality, future generations are likely to see the General as he was idealized in the vaporous closing scene of *Patton*, the movie: a lone, quixotic figure strolling with his fierce-looking (but gentle?) bull terrier, through a landscape dominated by a single windmill. A maligned hero. A good man, tragically out of his time.

To some extent, *Lines of Fire* may counteract the tendencies of time to blur, of Hollywood to oversimplify. Lest the hero and his thinking become altogether fantasized, we must remind ourselves of *all* that Patton stood for. To this end, he freely offered his war poems. They are precisely as "terrible" as the General wanted them to be. They are, in fact, "bad" poems – inelegant, violent, less the words of a poet than the unsheathed expressions of his "warrior soul." While Patton's verses are chilling testimonials to the "manly virtues" that he believed war engendered, they are also important autobiographical fragments, providing unmistakable cues to his mind and public mystique. And they go far toward answering Martin Blumenson's fundamental question: "What manner of man was this who took equal pleasure and pride in writing a poem and in killing an enemy soldier with his pistol?"[40]

---

39. Although Patton definitely is a role model for West Point Cadets and cadre, Colonel Turner notes that the General does not outshine other commanders such as Eisenhower, Bradley and MacArthur: "Each had his own unique style and traits that are worthy of emulation in leadership training." Letter, Colonel Robert A. Turner to Carmine A. Prioli, February 2, 1989.

40. Blumenson, I, p. 4.

EDITORIAL NOTE

Because he was dyslexic, General Patton's spelling was extremely erratic. I have, therefore, corrected words that seemed to have been unintentionally misspelled. At times I have also added punctuation where it was necessary to clarify the meaning of a line or stanza. Where two or more versions of a poem exist, I have chosen the latest version if a chronology of composition could be determined. In nearly all of the poems, the year of composition is available and appears on the right at the end of each text. Quite a few poems accompanied letters that the General wrote to his wife, and in these instances we have the exact date of composition. I have presented this information in the introductions that precede those poems. Where I could not ascertain a date of composition using either internal or external evidence, "n.d." (no date) follows the poem. Where I have speculated on a date of composition, I have placed a question mark next to the year. If a poem was published during Patton's lifetime, the year of publication follows on the left.

Although about a dozen of General Patton's poems have appeared in scattered biographies and in a few wartime magazines, *Lines of Fire* marks the first time that nearly all of his verses have been assembled in a single volume. Unless otherwise noted, all poems and quotations are from the unpublished letters and memoirs in the Patton Papers at the Library of Congress or the Patton Collection at the U.S. Military Academy Library.

C.A.P.

Graduation photo
U.S. Military Academy at West Point, 1909.
U.S. Army photo
Courtesy of the Patton Museum

I

1903 - 1917

WEST POINT AND MEXICO

We look upon the lengthened scroll of time
And Croesas is eclipsed by Bonaparte
What name of Milton, Dante or Shakespeare
May dare to stand with Caesar in the heart?

"To War"
Cadet George S. Patton, Jr.

A TOAST

[The manuscript version of "A Toast" displays the year 1903, thus identifying it as the earliest extant specimen of Patton's verse. It was probably composed while Patton was a cadet at the Virginia Military Institute. After one year at VMI, he was admitted to the United States Military Academy at West Point where in 1905 Beatrice Ayer–later Mrs. Patton–requested a sampling of his poetry. He responded with the first two stanzas of this poem, eight thumping lines in praise of old-fashioned carnage "In the days when war was war." Cadet Patton was his own severest critic, judging the piece in an accompanying letter as "worthless."[1] But he then carefully transcribed the poem into his notebook and added a third stanza.[2]]

>Oh! here's to the snarl of the striving steel
>When eye met eye on the foughten field[3]
>And the life went out with the entering steel
>In the days when war was war.
>
>And here's to the men who fought and strove
>And parried and hacked and thrust and clove
>Who fought for honor and fought for love
>In the days when war was war.

---

1. Blumenson, I, p. 270.

2. George S. Patton, Jr., "West Point Notebook," Patton Papers, Box 6, Library of Congress.

3. Possibly borrowed from Henry V's description of the battle of Agincourt as "this glorious and well-foughten field." See Shakespeare's *Henry V*, IV, vii, 18.

> Oh! here's to the maids for whom they fought
> For whom they strove, of whom they thought
> The maids whose love they nobly sought
> In the days when war was war.

1903-1905

THE FIVE STAGES OF CADET LIFE

[On June 16, 1904, Patton entered the United States Military Academy at West Point. He spent the next two months in field exercises, and by September he and the entering class were back in their barracks preparing for their academic studies. In November they had reached the two-hundred day countdown to the year's end in June, an occasion celebrated by each plebe's delivering a speech at dinner satirizing upper classmen. In the poem, for example, "Windy Jim" is the nickname of Jonathan M. Wainwright who was Cadet Sergeant Major for the 1904-05 academic year.[4]

In a letter to Beatrice, whom he would marry five years later, Patton said that he tried to imitate Shakespeare's "Seven Ages of Man," but substituted the five stages of cadet life. The result was among the first of many poems that Patton would compose and present to groups of military men. He described "The Five Stages of Cadet Life" as "a very poor attempt," but, he added, "it made most of the men laugh and that was all they wanted."[5]]

> "These lines attempt the gift to give us
> To see ourselves as others see us."[6]

---

4. Patton's friendship with Wainwright—whose career ended with the surrender of Bataan in 1942—persisted throughout their lives.

5. Blumenson, I, p. 105. In Shakespeare's *As You Like It*, the melancholy Jacques delineates the seven ages of man in his famous "All the world's a stage" soliloquy: infant, schoolboy, lover, soldier, judge, old fool, and senile dotard (II, vii). See also "The Life of a Cadet," p. 6.

6. In a handwritten note added later, Patton wrote: "I prefaced [this] speech with this altered quotation." Patton Papers, Box 60, Library of Congress. The original lines are in

First comes the youth who'd feign a soldier be
And doffs his cits to don the cadet grey.
Little he knows the woes that him await
When first he enters his hoped-for state.

Then comes the Plebe, of mortals he's the first
Into the gates of servitude to burst
With joy and zeal.
But e'er he has been at West Point a day
Though grey his dress, his hair is doubly grey.

For scarce he enters through that fateful door
E'er the fierce "Yearling"[7] jumps him from before.
While from the poop[8] with mighty belch and roar
Old "Windy Jim" doth grieve his patience sore.

A year has passed—the Yearling doth appear
Who looks on all Plebeans with a sneer.
Though he a Plebe was scarce three weeks ago
He now attempts to fill new Plebes with woe.
Does he succeed—let Heaven be the judge;
For all his noise, do any shoulders[9] budge?

And then the Second class man—look on him
For there's no creature which doth walk or swim
More sadly great or more serenely calm
'Twere far beneath such, any Plebe to harm.

'Tis only the Yearlings whom these try to show
How little of West Point they really know.
And now we reach the final stage of all
And gaze upon first class men great and small.

Though sometimes when at riding they most look
Like bobbing cork upon a rushing brook
Yet future bulwarks of our nation they
Will soon put on the blue and doff the grey.[10]

1904

Robert Burns' "To a Louse": "Oh was some power the giftie gie us / To see oursels as others see us!"

    7. A reference to cadets who have completed their first year. Also a pun on a year-old racehorse.

    8. The cadet yearbook (*The Howitzer*) for 1909 defines the "poop deck" as the "Tactical observatory balcony of Cadet Guard-house on which the O.C. [Cadet Officer in Charge] stands and harvests skins." "Skins" are delinquency reports, now synonymous with "gigs."

    9. A pun on "soldiers."

    10. When Patton wrote this poem, army dress uniforms were blue. Today they are green, but formal blue uniforms are still worn on special occasions.

THE LIFE OF A CADET

[Patton's next attempt at describing cadet life came a year later as he approached his twentieth birthday. Because he failed mathematics, Cadet Patton was repeating his first year and, in his own estimation, his life had so far amounted to nothing. Counting the time (1903-1904) he spent as a lower classman at VMI, he was in his third year as a plebe. Patton's mental depression deepened in October, 1905, when his hopes for playing football were dashed after he broke his right arm in practice. Sidelined in sports, he turned his attention towards writing poetry, but even these efforts were rejected by *The Howitzer*, West Point's cadet yearbook.

All in all, it amounted to "a pretty dull season" for Patton, whose disillusionment is evident in these lines that he sent to his father. "In the first place this is not connected," he wrote, "and in the second it is, I fear, not poetry. It was a by-product of my pen as I tried to write the seven ages of man. I am not going to turn it in, but thought that you might like to see it."[11] Mr. Patton's evaluation of the poem has not survived, but having earlier instructed his son to "school yourself to meet defeat and failure without bitter-ness...as becomes a man and a gentleman,"[12] he would certainly have disapproved of the poem's self-pitying tone.]

> And now we sing not of the stage of life
> But of that stage of which there is no counterpart on earth,
> The stages of the life of a cadet.
>
> First there's the boy
> Unapt by nature he for aught of hardship
> Yet his early mind perverted by untruthful literature
> He sees a picture of war glorified
> And longs to be a soldier.

---

11. Letter to "Papa," Patton Papers, Box 6, Library of Congress.

12. Blumenson, I, pp. 115-16.

He dreams of blood, of glory and of strife
And knows not blood is pain and glory but a bubble[13]
Which bursts when riper age has made his folly clear.

But why, alas, does knowledge come too late
That we who in our youth did know it not
Have wrecked our lives by learning too late?
For when the first bloom of our youth is gone
We're helpless in the grip of sterile habit
And cannot change, however much we strive.

Then though our souls rebel at servitude
He is our master even to the end
When we grown old, in harness die
And pass into a nothingness
But little less complete
Than that in which we lived.[14]

1905

BEATRICE

[Before she died in 1953, Mrs. Patton burned the General's love letters to her.[15] "Beatrice" is, therefore, one of only a few extant devotional verses Patton wrote for his wife. (See also "To Beatrice" and "To Your Picture," pp. 36 and 72.) Written when Patton was twenty-two years old, "Beatrice" is the earliest of his surviving love poems, and it shows the influence of the words and sentiments of at least two literary standbys. Shakespeare's Sonnet 18, "Shall I compare thee to a summer's day?" resonates in the first stanza, while the poem's distinction between physical and spiritual beauty recalls Dante's vision of "divine beauty" in his own

---

13. An allusion to Jacques' description of the soldier:
>Full of strange oaths, and bearded like the pard,
>Jealous in honour, sudden and quick in quarrel,
>Seeking the bubble reputation
>Even in the cannon's mouth. (*As You Like It*, II, vii.)

14. Patton here seems to have in mind the language of Shakespeare's *Macbeth* ("At least we'll die with harness on our back," V, vii, 52) and Keats' *Endymion* ("A thing of beauty is a joy forever...it will never/Pass into nothingness," I, 1-3).

15. Letter, Ruth Ellen Patton Totten to Carmine A. Prioli, September 4, 1988.

Beatrice. Certainly, the identical names of the real and the idealized women would not have escaped Patton's poetic scrutiny.]

> Should I compare you to the dawning day
> What day was e'er so beautiful as you?
> What colors of the dawn may hope to vie
> In their fresh pinkness to thy cheeks' fair hue?
>
> Or if with evening I compare thy face
> What stars fair shining that at evening rise
> Can in their sparkling loveliness compare
> To the pure splendor of thy lovely eyes?
>
> Show me the flower though it be passing fair
> That hath the velvet softness of thy cheek
> There never was a rose or lily blown
> That such divine perfection we might seek.
>
> Though such thy beauty that it doth surpass
> All else that nature hath fair or divine
> The beauty of thy face doth but reflect
> The hidden beauty that thy soul doth shine.

                                                              1908

TO WAR

[Written in 1909 when Patton was feeling "low" and "could see no hope of war,"[16] this ode laments the condition of mankind languishing, as he saw it, in the state of peace. It is the earliest poetic expression of Patton's belief in the principle of natural selection as applied to the evolution of law and human behavior. Our primitive battles with jungle apes led to the development of a civilization based on strength and the survival of the fittest. In Patton's view, the absence or conscious avoidance of war will lead to physical weakness, sensual indulgence, moral lassitude, and, in turn, to the erosion of the noblest and manliest qualities that have developed over the warring ages.

For Patton evidence of such erosion could be found even in the modern *practice* of war. In stanza three, for example, the lines decrying

---

16. Letter to "Papa and Mama," January 17, 1907, Patton Papers, Box 19, Library of Congress.

man's gliding up with "coward zeal" to hurl "Death and destruction on all standing nigh," probably refer to the growing use of balloons, dirigibles and airplanes for military purposes.[17] The impersonality of aerial warfare, of killing without actually fighting, offended Patton's sense of honor. By World War I, however, his arsenal of acceptable weapons included airplanes. In 1918 he viewed four hundred French warplanes, describing them as "wonderful" and aviators as men who do "the most wonderful things [killing Germans] in the quietest way."[18] Later, Patton himself learned to fly and his use of supporting air power and surveillance in World War II was a major factor contributing to the successes of his ground forces in France and Germany.]

> Oh! thou uncrowned mistress of all time[19]
> Since first man thought his brother man to slay
> Be not disgusted with our sudden state
> Nor fail in future with thy sons to stay.
>
> What though cursed striving over useless dross
> Has ruined half the soul God gave to man
> And made him as the swinish beasts that strive
> To swill their bellies with what e'er they can.
>
> What though the genius made for nobler things
> Has planned with coward zeal to scale the sky
> And gliding up unseen to dastard hurl
> Death and destruction on all standing nigh.
>
> Fear not great Mistress of the great in man
> There still exists and must until the end
> A strength which dastard cunning cannot quench
> Which avarice cannot as dollars spend.
>
> For which man lives and moves upon the sphere
> His path shall now as e'er be marked by war
> And he who on that path would leave a step
> Must guide him in accordance with thy law.

---

17. In 1908 the Wright brothers received their first contract for military aircraft. Although their prototype was unsuccessful, millions of dollars would soon be spent in Europe and Russia on all sorts of experiments with airborne machine guns, torpedoes and bombs.

18. Blumenson, I, pp. 396, 408.

19. Despite his later poetic appeals to a masculine "God of Battles," in his earlier years at least Patton visualized war as a muse-like female personage. In the spring of 1919, he had begun writing a book entitled *War As She Is*. Blumenson, I, p. 672.

For when the rich, the brilliant, and the great
Shall stand in nakedness before their God
How shall the glory of the gold or pin
Compare with that which from thy sword has flowed?

We look upon the lengthened scroll of time
And Croesas is eclipsed by Bonaparte
What name of Milton, Dante or Shakespeare
May dare to stand with Caesar in the heart?

Then grieve not Goddess of the nobly great
Though sad faced Peace overshadoweth the earth
Tis but the darkness of the coming day
And soon of war thy sons shall have no dearth.

And on every hand thou hearest as now
Men prate of Peace and all that it has done
Smile and remember were it not for Thee
Man still would slay his quarry with a stone.

For had not in the early dawn of life
Man warred with ape which ranked then with him
We still should swing in jungles by our tails
And chattering, leap with cries from limb to limb.

Had not the Christian stood against the Turk
And struggled glorious in bloody war
We now perchance should be debased as they
Looking with lust in all of good we saw.

Why then, oh Goddess, since times are as e'er
Should war be now so decadent and cursed?
Why should its good which oft has saved the world
Be now so much confounded with its worst?

Is it not possible that soon again
A worse than Turk shall raise his hand to slay?
And naught that all of glassy peace may do
Shall stop his hand until thou bidst him stay.

For though at times the world has been accursed
By greed of land, of gold, of worldly gain
Never has been such danger as may come
From senseless envy sown in common brain.

So true it is that in all walks of peace
Genius stands out but in one form exposed
While with the worshippers who follow war
Genius must stand in all her state disclosed.

1909

THE BRAVE WENT DOWN

[Late in his senior year at West Point, Patton visited Gettysburg with his classmates. It was his first trip to the historic battlefield, which he found "disappointing in its lack of size." Even Round Top, he noted in a letter to Beatrice, was "but a bump."[20] However unimpressed Patton was by its geographical scale, Gettysburg elicited – perhaps for the first time – the complex mystical connections that Patton perceived between fallen soldiers and nature, and between himself and his warrior-ancestors. "This evening after supper," he noted:

> I walked down alone to the scene of the last and fiercest struggle on Cemetery Hill. To get in a proper frame of mind, I wandered through the cemetery and let the spirits of the dead thousands laid in ordered rows sink deep into me. Then just as the sun sank behind South Mountains, I walked down to the scene of Pickett's great charge and, seated on a rock just where Olmstead[21] and two of my great uncles died,[22] I watched the wonder of the day go out.
> The sunset painted a dull red the fields over which the terrible advance was made and I could almost see them coming, growing fewer and fewer, while around and behind me stood calmly the very cannon that had so punished them. There were some quail calling in the trees nearby, and it seemed strange that they could do it where man had known his greatest and his last emotions. It was very wonderful, and no one came to bother me. I drank it in until I was quite happy. A strange pleasure, yet a very real one.[23]

---

20. Blumenson, I, p. 173

21. Patton's memory must have failed him here. The individual who led Virginian troops in a gallant charge against Union artillery was Brigadier General Lewis Armistead. No "Olmstead" is listed among Confederate officers who fought at Gettysburg.

22. Patton boasted of many illustrious military ancestors, but he was most proud of the seven Patton brothers who bore arms for the Confederacy during the Civil War. While all fought bravely, only one survived the war in sound health, and only one – Waller Tazewell Patton – was killed during Pickett's famous charge on July 3, 1863. Ashley Halsey, "Ancestral Gray Cloud Over Patton," *American History Illustrated* (March 1984), 42-48.

23. Blumenson, I, p. 173.

Even at the relatively young age of twenty-three, Patton sensed as "strange" his attraction to war and bloodshed. At the same time, he felt a certain regret: "I would like to have been there too,"[24] he wrote, feeling that he had missed one of mankind's most splendid events. Patton further expressed his thoughts in the following brief, untitled poem that anticipates his later practice of immersing himself in the ambience of ground made sacred by heroic strife.]

> The brave went down
> Without disgrace they leaped to ruin's red embrace
> They only heard fame's thunder wake
> And saw the dazzling sun burst break
> In smiles on glory's bloody face.[25]

1909

SERVANTS

[On April 7, 1910, Patton wrote "Servants" and two letters to Beatrice concerning their upcoming marriage, honeymoon and future living arrangements. Less than a year out of West Point, he was brimming with enthusiasm about his personal life, but was disgusted with his role as a "pot bound" soldier in a peacetime army, unappreciated and largely unsupported by its civilian leaders. Patton composed "Servants" to vent his feelings, and probably to entertain his fellow officers. It is the earliest poetic expression of his lifelong antipathy for journalists and politicians.[26]]

---

24. Blumenson, I, p. 173.

25. As the poem indicates, for Patton the brave "went down" at Gettysburg and were killed. Among his close acquaintances, he never concealed his utter contempt for survivors of great battles who, in his eyes, basked in the glory of their fallen comrades. Four years after his first visit, Patton was sent to do "policeman work" at Gettysburg, where survivors were celebrating the fiftieth anniversary of the battle. In one afternoon, he distributed nearly eight thousand blankets to the veterans, whom he described venomously as "a disgusting bunch, dirty and old....One old hound has been beating a drum ever since he got here." Blumenson, I, p. 255.

26. Despite his low regard for politicians, Patton was encouraging his father to run for the U. S. Senate. Blumenson, I, p. 203.

The servants of a nation that's unwarlike
And living in an age that knows not war
We sit and sadly wonder, how we ever came to blunder
Into thinking that we martial glory saw.

They say we are a necessary nuisance
And unto fat policemen us compare.
And when we think upon it we really must admit it,
For policing is our joy and our despair.

So we spend our time in hoping that all those who rank[27] us die
[So] that we shall all be generals in a day.
But the congressmen all fool us, and to sweet submission school us
And our increase simply vanishes away.

Some day our long delayed and expected war will come
And shall we get the credit? Heavens no!
The editors who rule us will as ever nicely fool us
The "malish"[28] will get the credit if they stay.

But they will probably leave us all alone to face the foe
Out numbered and out generaled by the "Press."
And when the Japs[29] have killed us and in trenches ten deep piled us
Perhaps the nation will remember this:

You can't have an army without soldiers
And soldiers ain't constructed in the shops
If you want to make them, you must first get and break them
And regulars ain't militia men nor cops.

1910

OH, YE FOOLISH HALF-GOD MORTALS

[On May 26, 1910, Lieutenant George S. Patton, Jr. married Beatrice Banning Ayer, the daughter of a wealthy and influential Boston businessman. After an elaborate wedding and festive reception, the Pattons left for a European honeymoon. One of their first stops was Tintagel in Cornwall where, Patton noted in his diary, they "read a lot about Arthur," whom the

---

27. Outrank.

28. A colloquial army term ("maleesh") referring to those with attitudes of indifference or slackness. It originated in the regular army's disdain for the militia (pronounced "milishy" but often shortened to "milish"), local troops called out to fight only during great emergencies.

29. See also "The Rulers," p. 22.

local people spoke of "as if he were still here."[30] This popular belief in Arthur's continued existence and the castle itself reinvigorated Patton's childhood dreams and his spiritual connection with figures from medieval romance, inspiring him to record the following poem. It foreshadows themes of mysticism and reincarnation that Patton would develop in poems such as "Ouija" and "Through a Glass, Darkly" (pp. 104 and 118).

Later events indicate that Tintagel's "Elfin music" continued to play in Patton's ear when he exercised his Arthurian fantasies even as an older man. In 1935 he sailed from California to Hawaii in his fifty-two foot schooner, *Arcturus*, and four years later, in an elaborate costume he designed and assembled himself, Patton paraded at a fashionable Washington military pageant dressed as King Arthur. Mrs. Patton rode at his side as the stately Guinevere, and the royal couple came equipped with horses and an entourage of jesters. This masquerade was a playful expression of the General's fantasies, the visible manifestation of sentiments that found more serious outlets in his leadership and his poetry.]

> Oh, ye foolish half-God mortals
> Making mock of Faun and Fay;
> 'Tis in minds and not in caverns,
> Now as e'er our crafts we play.
>
> Still the minds of untaught children
> Summon up from out the grove
> Voices in the voiceless forest
> Elfin music in a cove.
>
> With your learned modern science
> You may prove that we are dead,
> Yet e'en now we live among you
> As in ages that are sped.
>
> When you sit by the sea shore
> And your soul runs loosely back,
> 'Long the path of countless ages
> That the soul alone may track,
>
> Then ye shudder and look backward
> Thinking now as long ago
> That a goblin lurks beside you
> Or a fay her horn doth blow.
>
> 1910

---

30. "My Trip Abroad," Patton Papers, Box 1, Library of Congress.

BILLY THE OLD TROOP HORSE

[Patton dated these lines November 28, 1910, and at the bottom he inscribed: "Written in great melancholy at the desertion of his wife."[31] This was a tongue-in-cheek reference to the couple's spending their first Thanksgiving apart, while Beatrice visited her ailing father in Boston. Patton remained at Ft. Sheridan where he passed a rousing holiday with fellow officers, dining on the meal for six that his wife had prepared before she left.

In a letter he wrote earlier in 1910, Patton admitted that he was "inclined to show emotion,"[32] and this poem reveals the sentimental streak that remained with him throughout his lifetime. It also indicated his regard for beasts and men who have labored nobly for their country. Critical of a thankless, impersonal system that rewards duty well-performed with neglect and indifference, the poem indicated the moral decline of the peacetime U.S. Army.

Despite congressional efforts to "Americanize" the enlisted ranks, one third to one fourth of the army's recruits continued to be immigrants, a sizeable portion of whom were drawn from populous northeastern cities like New York and Boston.[33] In Patton's view, these recruits not only made poor soldiers: they were throwbacks to remote periods of human evolution. (See also "The City of Dreadful Light," p. 115.) Thus, the once-proud Billy dies ignobly, but he is free from the abuses of "that dago Joe," a heartless and ignorant army teamster.]

---

31. Patton Papers, Box 60, Library of Congress.

32. In this letter to his mother, Patton confessed: "I...am not over bold and am inclined to show emotion – a most unmilitary trait." Blumenson, I, p. 199.

33. Edward M. Coffman, *The Old Army: A Portrait of the American Army in Peacetime, 1784-1898* (New York: Oxford University Press, 1986), pp. 328-31.

Inspected and condemned! Ah, God,
    because I was not made of iron.
For years at practice, march, parade, and drill,
I bore my rider faithfully and well,
    doing what duty any horse can do,
And without biting, kicking, or sore back;
Until at last old age came and made
    a stiffening in my every joint.

But I was treated well, placed in the band
    and given every care that they could give.
Until at last the fatal day came round,
When my stiff limbs could not maintain their pace
To do their duty even with the band.
I tried and trying fell, breaking my rider's arm.

How can I blame them then if the next day with
    great regret they let me be condemned?
Even the blacksmith, when he placed the iron,
Scarcely did more than burn away the hair.
Yet that I.C.[34] has broken my old heart,
And as I stand here hitched by wire and rope
    into this crazy cart,
In which I drag the soldiers' laundry,
    how I long to die.

I who, when guidon,[35] never needed spur!
I who have paced my regiment for miles
    at every gate,
Here in a cart belabored by a jay
    who knows not girth from stirrup
And scarce can speak my master's language.
Yes, I whose sleek round sides
    have been a squadron's pride,
A rat-tailed nag whose bones stick
    through the skin with lack of food,
And all because I was too strong to die
    on the bleak stretches of Montana snow,
Because I could withstand at any pace
    the burning deserts of New Mexico.

Truly the mighty nation that I served,
    served with my youth and strength
Should feel ashamed to see her servant
    brought to my estate,
Yet pension men who work not half so well.

---

34. Abbreviation for "Inspected and Condemned."

35. The small flag identifying a cavalry unit.

Ah! here they come, my comrades!
    Marching past, at a round trot,
Another guidon horse bearing the flag
    that used to be my pride.
I'll follow! But this load? The traces break!
I head the troop, the squadron once again,

But starving, first I falter; then I'm down!
And from above with new coltish eyes,
    see comrades gather round my broken form,
And whispering say, "Yes, that's sure Billy's main
Thank God he's gone and left that dago Joe."

    1910

EPITAPH TO A HORSE

[In the tradition of popular epitaphs, the author of this tribute is listed as "Unknown." However, the sentimental flavor and language of the poem — and its inclusion with other typescripts of the General's verses — suggest that the poet was Patton.]

Soft lies the turf on these who find their rest
Beneath our common Mother's ample breast.
Unstained by meanness, avarice, or pride
They never cheated and they never lied.

They never intrigued a revolt to displace,
They ran, but never betted on the race.
Content with honest sport and simple food
Boundless in faith and love and gratitude.

Happy the man, if there be any such,
Of whom his epitaph can say as much.

    Unknown.

    n.d.

2nd Lt. Patton practicing hurdles for the 1912 Olympics, where he competed in the Modern Pentathlon, finishing fifth overall.
Photo courtesy of the Patton Museum

MARCHING IN MEXICO

[Although written in 1919, "Marching in Mexico" recalls Patton's experiences in 1916 as a young officer serving with the 8th Calvary during the Punitive Expedition against Pancho Villa. Patton became a sensation in the United States after he led a small group of men in a dramatic gunfight against a band of Villa's outlaws. When the smoke and the dust settled at the Rubio Ranch, three Mexicans were dead, two killed by Patton himself. One of the casualties turned out to be Colonel Julio Cárdenas, a key man in Villa's guerilla campaign. Patton then draped the bodies across the hood of his car and returned to headquarters where he won the admiration of John J. Pershing, his commanding general.

Because he used automobiles during this maneuver, Patton is credited with initiating motorized warfare in the U. S. Army. In retrospect, this must have seemed fitting when, two years later, he would organize and command the 304th Tank Brigade during the St. Mihiel and, for a time, The Meuse-Argonne Offensives.

Lieutenant Patton's brief but violent encounter with the Mexicans was tremendously important to him personally. It was the first time his warrior pedigree had been truly tested. He had come out on top in a fair fight against a tough and elusive foe. The bloodletting was, therefore, an invigorating experience for him, but it was not nearly enough to satisfy his longing for sustained combat. Apart from the Rubio Ranch showdown, Patton's duty in Mexico was, on the whole, dreary, dusty and boring. All the while, a glorious war was raging in Europe and he wanted to be part of it. Because peace and neutrality efforts in the United States had so far kept him from doing so, in 1916 Patton wrote a half dozen poems in which he waged a personal war in poetry against Woodrow Wilson and, as he saw them, the misguided or cowardly pacifists who were working to keep America out of the real fighting. In the process, these individuals were also denying him the opportunity to further demonstrate his warrior status.

[Commenting on "Marching in Mexico," Mrs. Patton wrote: "A great picture. One of my favorites."[36]]

> The column winds on snakelike,
> Through blistering, treeless spaces;
> The hovering gray-black dustclouds
> Tint in ghoulish shades our faces.
>
> The sweat in muddied bubbles,
> Trickles down the horses' rumps;
> The saddles creak, the gunboots chafe,
> The swinging holster bumps.
>
> At last the "Halt" is sounded,
> The outpost trots away;
> The lines of tattered pup-tents rise –
> We've marched another day.
>
> The rolling horses raise more dust,
> While from the copper skies
> Like vultures, stooping on the slain,
> Come multitudes of flies.
>
> The irate cooks their rites perform
> Like pixies round the blaze;
> The smoking greasewood stings our eyes,
> Sunscorched for countless days.
>
> The sun dips past the western ridge,
> The thin dry air grows cold;
> We shiver through the freezing night,
> In one thin blanket rolled.
>
> The night wind stirs the cactus,
> And sifts the sand o'er all;
> The horses squeal, the sentries curse,
> The lean coyotes call.

1919

VALOR

[At the end of the typescript of this poem, Patton noted that it was "The result of reading in the papers the utterances of Ford and such scum."[37] He was referring to the automaker-industrialist, Henry Ford, who in

---

36. "Marching in Mexico," Patton Collection, U. S. Military Academy Library.

37. "Valor," Patton Papers, Box 60, Library of Congress.

December, 1915, sailed to Europe with a peace delegation in an unsuccessful effort to end World War I. Ford's objective was to get the armies out of the trenches and back to their homes by Christmas.

"Valor" was one of Patton's poetic responses to Ford and to the declaration of neutrality by Woodrow Wilson, who had tried to keep the United States out of the conflict by appealing to Americans to be impartial in thought as well as in action. Never impartial toward anything that involved the chance to fight, Patton was disgusted with Wilson's policy.

In "Valor" the line describing the "blackest" sin as "pride which will not fight" is clearly a reference to the President's widely publicized speech of May 10, 1915. In an address to fifteen thousand listeners crowded into Philadelphia's Convention Hall, Wilson observed that "There is such a thing as a man being too proud to fight."[38] Less than a week after Wilson made his speech, Patton wrote to his father: "In any other country or age that pride has always been called another name."[39]]

> When all the hearts are opened
> And all the secrets known
> When guile and lies are banished
> And subterfuge is gone
>
> When God rolls up the curtain
> And hidden truths appear
> When the ghastly light of Judgement Day
> Brings past and present near...
>
> Then shall we know what once we knew
> Before wealth dimmed our sight
> That of all the sins, the blackest is
> The pride which will not fight.
>
> The meek and pious have a place
> And necessary are,
> But valor pales their puny rays
> As does the sun a star.
>
> What race of man since time began
> Has ever yet remained
> Who trusted not its own right hand
> Or from brave deeds refrained?

---

38. Arthur S. Link. ed., *The Papers of Woodrow Wilson*, vol. 33 (Princeton, N.J.: Princeton University Press, 1980), p. 149.

39. Blumenson, I, p. 289.

Yet, spite the fact for ages known
And by all lands displayed
We still have those who prate of peace
And say that war is dead.

Yes, vandals rise who seek to snatch
The laurels from the brave
And dare defame heroic dead
Now filling hero graves.

They speak of those whose love,
Like Christ's, exceeds the lust of life
As murderers slain to no avail
A useless sacrifice.

With infamy without a name
They mock our fighting youth
And dare decry great hearts who die
Battling for right and truth.

Woe to the land which, heeding them,
Lets avarice gain the day
And trusting gold its rights to hold
Lets manly might decay.

Let us, while willing yet for peace,
Still keep our valor high
So when our time of battle comes
We shall not fear to die.

Make love of life and ease be less
Make love of country more
So shall our patriotism be
More than an empty roar.

For death is nothing, comfort less
Valor is all in all
Base nations who depart from it
Shall sure and justly fall.

1916

THE RULERS

[Written in 1916, "The Rulers" reveals Patton's distaste for midwestern populists, congressional "Rulers from the corn belt," who, he believed, were more concerned with their own special interests and reforms than with American military preparedness. World War I was underway in Europe and Patton was eager for active U. S. involvement. Additionally, he was convinced that Japan intended to invade the western United States, a fear especially strong in California, his home state, where resentment against Oriental migration had been growing for years.

Although he later claimed to be apolitical, in 1916 Patton was deeply conservative, wealthy, and at odds with the progressivism of the period. Utterly contemptuous of "the masses," Patton feared that the end of Western civilization was at hand, and warned that the "deluge" was certain to come. "It is everywhere the effort of the inefficient to pull down the great, [it is] mob courage," he wrote in 1912. "People who have money had best enjoy it for they may not have it long. The many headed beast called 'the people' is howling for its envious hordes. It will get [what it wants] and then stupid with gorging will be chained as before." Then he added solemnly, "I hope I help make that chain."[40]

In "The Rulers" Patton prophesies a "day of reckoning" when the army—untrained and ill-equipped—will fail to expel alien invaders. The rulers will then be replaced by anarchic mobs until "a single man" arises to quell them and, with an iron hand, restores peace. Then, only "fools" will talk of equal rights. Neither Patton's poems nor his letters indicate specifically whom he thought this superman might be, but when he wrote of his wish to be "a dictator or a president,"[41] it is clear that he saw himself as physically and ideologically compatible with either role.]

> The Rulers of the people
> Debated vaporously
> Enacting laws which should reform
> The earth and sky and sea.
>
> No longer should the angels
> Continuously play
> Eight hours set the limit
> Even of celestial day.[42]

---

40. Letter to "Beatrice," September 1, 1912, Patton Papers, Box 7, Library of Congress.

41. Letter to his parents, January 17, 1909, Blumenson, I, p. 161. See also Patton's letter (p. 239) to his father-in-law, September 14, 1912, in which he stated "politics is what I am after...."

42. In 1912 Congress passed an eight-hour-day law for all federal workers. The Ford Motor Company did the same for its workers in 1914.

Yet the fishes in the ocean
Must abide by man made rules
And no longer stay congested
In those large unhealthy schools.[43]

While on the earth the Savior
Would surely feel at home
Where laws which banish every vice
Make every virtue come.[44]

Meantime to soothe the folks at home
They voted many a dollar
To make a Federal Building
In the woods at Turtle Hollow.

To build a pier in Duck Creek
To dredge an open bay
To pension veterans' grandsons
And to raise their own poor pay.

Yet while they cut the "Mellon"
And reformed the human soul
The buildings that they sat in
Trembled to the cannon's roll.

They knew the army had no guns
It also had no votes.
And the Rulers from the corn belt
Aren't interested in boats.

At last the day of reckoning came
The million farmers rose.
To battle? No! They packed their things
And fled before their foes.

They saw their gunless army die
At each Thermopylae
They saw an alien rule their states
That fringe the western sea.

Then rose the cry which Tiber heard
From all the windy pack
And "Those in rear cried 'Forward!'

---

43. Perhaps a reference to congressional resolutions in 1916 aimed at restricting American travel abroad. These were part of the effort to keep the United States out of the European war by preventing Americans from sailing on ships that might be sunk by the Germans.

44. In 1916 the Prohibition Party had its own presidential candidate and the Anti-Saloon League had influenced the passage of "dry" laws in twenty-four states.

While those in front cried 'Back!'"[45]

They found that money stays not steel
That credit stops not shell
So both were impotent to check
That tide of "Yellow Hell."

The Rulers of the people
Debated feverishly
Enacting laws that every man
Must serve on land or sea.

They builded no more buildings
They let the fishes school
They let the angels play at will
They settled down to rule.

They raised a mighty army
And set it forth untrained
The desert drank the bloody dew
But not a pass was gained.

The people then displaced them
And sought to rule instead
The desert was new watered
But the "Yellow Menace" stayed.

A single man displaced the mob
They welcomed him with cheers
Through blood he gained the sea shore
But it took him twenty years.

The land is once more peaceful
The people no more rule
And he who talks of equal rights
Is written down a fool.

1916

L'ENVOI

[A poetic "envoi" (send off) was a short concluding stanza used by French medieval poets as a kind of post-script or summation. The form was revived and expanded in the nineteenth century by English poets, including Scott, Southey and Swinburne. Because of the military associations of "envoi"

---

45. Paraphrased from one of Patton's favorite poems, Thomas Babington Macaulay's *Lays of Ancient Rome* (1842), *Horatius*, st. 50. The original reads, "But those behind cried 'Forward!' / And those before cried 'Back!'"

(it is also French for "military dispatch") or "envoy," the form was popular among poets like Kipling and his later Canadian counterpart, Robert W. Service, who often concluded a series or volume of poems with a verse entitled "L'Envoi."

Patton left no indication where he intended to place his own "L'Envoi," but the poem appears among his earliest and most virulent commentaries on the "priceless benefit" of war.]

> When the last great battle is finished
> And the last great general shall fall,
> When the roar of the mighty guns is dumb
> As the kiss of the nickeled ball,
> When the screams of the dying that mixed
> With the shout that the living give out
> As they rush on the foe,
> When the mixed noise of an army in flight
> The gasp and the curse and the shouting are low,
> When soldiers have ceased to struggle,
> When war is raged with the tongue,
> When men are praised for cowardice
> And men for bravery hung,
> When honor and virtue and courage
> Are fled like departing day
> As the cursed shape of eternal peace
> Comes up on the evening gray,
> When money is God and Lord of all
> And liars alone have weight,
> When the road to heaven is barred with gold
> And wide yawns Hell's black gate –
> Then those who live in servile chains
> To filthy lucre slaves
> Ah, how they will yearn for the soldier's life
> And for the hero's grave,
> And will say as they sadly think of it:
> War was a priceless benefit
> Although a sacrifice.

1916?

2nd Lt. Patton, the U.S. Army's first Master of the Sword, executing mounted saber exercises at Fort Riley, Kansas, in 1913.
U.S. Army photo
Courtesy of the Patton Museum

THE CAVE MAN

[A vivid example of Patton's belief in the idea that modern civilization has its roots in prehistoric strife, "The Cave Man" was written while Patton was serving with Pershing in Mexico. A shorter version of eleven stanzas, entitled "Might–Right," concluded an article on Patton, making this his first published poem. Headlined "George S. Patton, Jr., Soldier, Diplomat, Poet," the article and poem appeared in the *Los Angeles Graphic* on June 23, 1917. It was effusive in its praise for this "Los Angeles boy, born and bred," who recited for the author several "well made poems...full of broad philosophy; some humorous, some serious."[46]

Patton rarely spoke highly of his own poetry, but he seemed especially proud of "The Cave Man." When he sent it to Beatrice the previous September, Patton noted that he had shown it to General Pershing, "who read it over twice and was quite impressed." Patton then instructed his wife to try and get it published "in some good magazine."[47] A few years later when Patton was editing this poem for publication, he noted that it was composed in Mexico "on a crackerbox," and added that it took "about thirty minutes."[48]]

*When man in the dark beginning
The brutish form set by
He stood alone in the forest
To conquer or to die.

At first he had no classmates
But each for himself stood forth
And strove with the mammoth and aurochs
'Midst the ice of the cruel north.

*His only motive was hunger
Of the belly or of lust
His only Right was his hairy Might
Courage his only trust.

---

46. See "Scrapbook," Patton Papers, Box 69, Library of Congress.
47. Letter to "Beatrice," September 15, 1916, Patton Papers, Box 8, Library of Congress.
48. "The Cave Man," Patton Collection, U. S. Military Academy Library.
* Asterisks indicate stanzas that were published as "Might–Right."

*So he learned that to fight was noble
So he learned that to shirk was base
Thus he conquered the creatures one and all
And founded a warrior race.

*He fought with beasts and reptiles
When the coal fields were forests dark
And he vanquished them, not by Justice
But by brawn and a mighty heart.

*But suppose for a moment this man of might
Had been of the Pacifist clay
And had crooned to tigers of ethical right
Or had begged of the wolves fair play.

Where now would our civilization be
With its so-called peace through right
With its feeble laws obeyed for love
And its fear of the justice of might?

Instead of being the lord of life
In city or town or farm
Man, naked, would skip through the endless woods
And hide in the leaves from harm.

*When the cave man sat in his stinking lair
With his low-browed mate hard by
Gibbering the while he sank his teeth
In a new-killed reindeer's thigh,

*What would he have thought, could his foggy brain
Have pictured our hapless day,
When craven souls of drivelling fools
Should 'habit our human clay?

*When bastards bred of Fear by Greed
Should preach to kindred slaves,
That Right may stand of its self alone
And need not Might to save?

Whose women prate of eras new
Whence vice and lust are fled
Where wordy laws, unbacked by force
Hold sway o'er spirits dead.

*They speak but lies, these sexless souls
Lies born of fear of strife
And nurtured in soft indulgence
They know not War is Life.

*They dare not recognize the fact
Though writ in letters red
That man has progressed now as e'er
By blood which man has shed.

Since first the clans were gathered
There's been no law but Might
And when men saw they must obey
They said such laws were right.

Yet dreamers spawned in idleness
Fearing the test of war
And howl in puny petulance
And prate of forceless law.

*Dreading the truth plain written
In wrecks of empires lost,
That those who trust to words, not Force
As slaves shall pay the cost.

1916

TO WILSON

[As he did with all of his early poems, Patton sent this one to his wife and added: "The rainy season is over and the wind and dust is back again. It was terrible today and naturally not good for hay fever. I felt so low that I wrote the enclosed effusion."[49] Patton's depression was brought on not only by the weather and his allergy, but by the U. S. Army's languishing in Mexico while Europe was embroiled in war. Patton's greatest fear was that the conflict would end before he had his chance to fight.

Patton's ill-humor is obvious in this poetic tirade which, with all of its vicious sarcasm, did not "half express [his] feelings for Wilson." Although Patton noted that his real views were "not fit to print," he planned to publish this poem "late in November" of 1916, after his father's senatorial campaign. The poem, however, was never printed, even after the President was reelected, and despite the fact that Mr. Patton lost his own bid for public office. No doubt Patton was dissuaded from publishing "To Wilson" by his father, who had supported Wilson and his policy of neutrality toward the European war. And although the elder Patton always encouraged the literary efforts of his son, he probably found this poem coarse and amateurish.

Whatever Mr. Patton may have thought of "To Wilson," his son certainly liked it, especially the last verse, which he then considered "the best

---

49. Letter to "Darling Beat," September 20, 1916, Patton Papers, Box 20, Library of Congress.

piece of expression [I] ever got off." At the same time, he also jokingly confessed, "If I took the best verses out of all the stuff I have written, I might get up a good poem."[50]]

> Ah! God how much we hate this place
> No one shall ever know
> Shut off from those we hold most dear
> Unsought by any foe.
>
> Choked by the dust-ladened winds
> Drowned by the rains which fall
> Damned by the fever-bearing flies
> We live yet suffer all.
>
> If our own country we did serve
> Or ease another's woe
> There is not any one of us
> These sufferings would forego.
>
> But knowing as all of us do
> That we no end can gain
> Except to let a snivelling fool
> A few more votes obtain.
>
> A fool with whose uncertainty
> The weather vane can't vie
> A knave whose courage is far less
> Than the startled hares that fly.
>
> Hence pray we to all-seeing God
> To damn for us this man
> Who prating of great policies
> Cannot conceive one plan.
>
> We know, Oh God, that you are just
> And great your wisdom is
> So think us not presumptuous when
> We ask for Wilson this.
>
> Let him be sent to Mexico
> His escort made of flies
> Let him be shrivelled by the cold
> Of the wind which never dies.
>
> Let him forever gasp for breath
> In dust which has no end
> To gnaw on him eternally
> Ten million vermin send.

---

50. Letter to "Darling Beat," September 20, 1916, Patton Papers, Box 20, Library of Congress.

Let the disease[51] which like a plague
Stalks shameless in these lands
Attack and rot his vitals
So he withers where he stands.

We know, just God, that what we urge
For vengeance is but weak
We trust that You will give him more
But this, at least, we seek –

That he shall know the utter woe
Ten thousand men have known
And feel that while he suffers all
He never can atone.

For making soldiers play the part
Of dogs who will not fight
Of dogs, who fearful not to growl
Fear far too much to bite.

1916

ETERNAL PEACE

[In 1795 the German philosopher, Immanuel Kant, published an essay delineating a political program that would make it possible for men to live with each other without the fear or threat of war. Entitled *Eternal Peace* or *Perpetual Peace* (*Zum ewigen Frieden*), the work was reprinted many times, and provided Woodrow Wilson with a manifesto for his League of Nations. Kant prescribed rules for an ideal world-state governed according to international law and principles of republicanism. In such a state, standing armies would be rendered obsolete and subsequently abolished as each man, vested with a kind of world citizenship, enjoyed conditions of "universal hospitality."[52]

"Eternal Peace" is one of Patton's caustic responses to Kant's proposal and to the political agendas of its modern champions like the International Peace Parliament. (See also "The Curse of Kant" and "The End of War," pp.

---

51. Probably dysentery.

52. Lewis White Beck, ed., *Perpetual Peace* (Indianapolis and New York: Bobbs-Merrill, 1957), p. 20.

34 and 62.) The existence of such groups infuriated Patton, who heckled their objective as "Infernal Peace." Like many others of his era, Patton was convinced that the pacifists' views were hopelessly – and perilously – divorced from the reality that war was a permanent fact of human life. Unlike many others, however, Patton was gambling that his "destiny" was intricately tied up in war, which he saw as "a very beautiful intellectual contest."[53]

In a note he appended to this poem, Patton later remarked: "Time of writing about twenty minutes."[54]]

> Since the ancient Christian zealots
> With an early Christian smile
> Beat out the brains of heathens
> In a very righteous style
>
> Down the passion-clouded ages
> To the Inquisition's time
> Have all sorts of other bigots
> Practiced every sort of crime.
>
> The Round Heads[55] with intolerance
> Lopped the curly heads off peers
> Singing psalms the while they rotted
> Stuck aloft on grisly spears.
>
> And the pious folk of Salem
> Burned their witches with great glee
> Fully confident that Heaven
> Took delight such sights to see.[56]
>
> So today in equal folly
> Do our Pacifists assail

---

53. Letter to "Beatrice," April 26, 1908, Blumenson, I, p. 145.

54. "The Pacifist," Patton Collection, U. S. Military Academy Library.

55. A member of Oliver Cromwell's Puritan party during the English Civil War (1642-1652). "Roundhead" was a derisive term referring to the Puritans' close-cropped hair, especially over the ears, in contrast to the wigs and long hair of the Cavaliers.

56. Patton here refers to the infamous witch trials that took place in Salem Village, Massachusetts, in 1692, when nineteen people were executed for practicing witchcraft. His reference to the convicted being burned is inaccurate. Although in seventeenth-century New England individuals were hanged for witchcraft, there are only two known instances of execution by burning, and neither of them was related to the crime of witchcraft. George F. Dow, *Every Day Life in the Massachusetts Bay Colony* (1935; rpt. New York: Dover, 1988), p. 210.

Those who still upholding honor
The Millenium[57] will not hail.

Yes, these last demented creatures
Seek with words to crucify
Those, who for their country's honor,
Still are not afraid to die.

Yet as surely as these others
Have at last been held to shame
So will future generations
Our poor Pacifists defame.

For a thousand years ahead of us
Will you as surely find
The world as full of passion
As a thousand years behind.

For mankind is just as warlike
As it was before the flood
And the clay which molds us moderns
Is the same old blood-soaked mud.

1916

THE CURSE OF KANT

[At the bottom of the typescript of this poem, Patton noted that it was "Written as a protest of all the 'gloom' appearing in the papers which is calculated to destroy the spirit of any army. Battle is only horrible to those who are afraid to fight."[58]]

The papers publish sob-stuff
And drool of the horrors of strife
They speak of the fallen as murdered
And lie about us and our life.

But we who are in it know better
There still is a glory to war
The death which one dies for Country
Is nobler than ever before.

The wolf which fights not for her litter
The man who resents not a blow

---

57. The thousand-year period of peace and the reign of Christ as prophesied in Revelations (20: 1-5).

58. "The Curse of Kant," Patton Collection, U. S. Military Academy Library.

The nation which makes mock of glory
Shall perish in limitless woe.

Men who have struggled as heroes
Men who have suffered and bled
Men who have frozen and hungered
Should be honored, living or dead.

But ours who have prated of ethics
And cringed at the sufferings of strife
Dishonor their land and their women
And the pains which have given them life.

The youth who dies for his country
But follows the teachings of God
Giving life that others may prosper
He treads as his Savior trod.

Then seek not in maudlin pity
To regret those nobly slain
Who die in their land's service
Have never lived in vain.

For those whose lives are spent in lust
Of ease or wealth or food
Whose souls have rotted e'er they died
Whose deaths have done no good.

For such set up your woeful howls
For such pour forth your prayers
The brave who dies needs not your sighs
Nor for your pity cares.

Let papers cease to mourn the lost
Mourn fights we do not gain
Instead of mulling o'er the dead
Enlist! Replace the slain.

1917

YOUTH

[On October 2, 1916, while working in his tent, Patton sustained first-degree burns about his face and hands when gasoline flew out of the lantern he was pumping. Sometime during the next several weeks while recuperating, he wrote this poem and "To Beatrice" which follows. At the bottom of the page, he described "Youth" as an "experiment with two rhymes per stanza."[59]]

>Since the unrecorded ages
>When man first hoarded food
>Has a countless line of sages
>Preached sheer folly to their brood.
>
>Preached and praised the art of saving
>For some future never known
>Putting off the day of spending
>Till the zest of youth is flown.
>
>Letting slip the joys which hundreds
>To the youthful would have brought
>Till in age they find that millions
>Cannot buy the joys they sought.
>
>Oh! how foolish and how wanton
>Is niggardness in youth
>And how sadly and how often
>Do the aged learn this truth.
>
>Then let us scorn the teaching
>Which bids us hoard today
>For the future is but shadows
>And the aged cannot play.
>
>So in thankfulness of living
>Let us spend while we are young
>For tomorrow is but grieving
>For the joys which then are gone.

1916

TO BEATRICE

[One of only a handful of extant devotional poems that Patton composed specifically for his wife (see also "Beatrice" and "To Your Picture," pp. 7 and 72), "To Beatrice" was written in 1916 as a substitute for the daily letter he usually wrote and sent to her. "There is no news," he scribbled at

---

59. "Youth," Patton Papers, Box 60, Library of Congress.

the bottom of the page, "so I wrote the above. It's not good, for I love you more than the confines of some verse admit of saying."[60]

Although the sentiments of "To Beatrice" may seem inflated, there is no doubt that Patton was entirely sincere when he spoke of Beatrice as his mainstay and inspiration. Theirs was a marriage based, in part, upon the medieval tradition of courtly love. From the time of their wedding, when the bride cut the cake with the groom's sword, an easy familiarity obtained between love and honor, between marriage vows and the martial spirit. If she was his "Dear Queen,"[61] he was surely her modern Knight. When Patton later received the Distinguished Service Cross for gallantry under fire in World War I, Beatrice wrote: "Georgie, you are the fulfillment of all the ideals of manliness and high courage & bravery I have always held for you,...And I have expected more of you than any one else in the world ever has or will." Patton copied this into his diary, adding: "I'm glad she likes me."[62]]

> Oh! loveliest of women
> What e'er I gain or do
> Is naught if in achieving
> I bring not joy to you.
>
> I know I often grieve you –
> All earthly folk are frail
> But if this grief I knowing wrought
> My life's desire would fail.
>
> The mandates of stern duty
> Oft take us far apart
> But space is impotent to check
> The heart which calls to heart.
>
> Perhaps by future hidden
> Some greatness waits in store[63]
> If so, the hope your praise to gain
> Shall make my efforts more.
>
> For victory apart from you
> Would be an empty gain

---

60. Letter to "Darling Beat," October 1916, Patton Papers, Box 60, Library of Congress.

61. Letter to "Beat," March 10, 1909, Patton Papers, Box 19, Library of Congress.

62. Blumenson, I, p. 669.

63. This was more than wishful thinking. Patton was convinced that he was destined to achieve greatness.

> A laurel crown you could not share
> Would be reward in vain.
>
> You are my inspiration
> Light of my brain and soul
> Your guiding love by night and day
> Will keep my valor whole.

1916

THE FLY

[In a letter to Beatrice on July 29, 1916, Patton wrote: "I enclose two disgusting poems I have composed. Tear them up." Next day, he wrote again saying: "On rereading those poems I am sorry I sent them to you. You will think me nasty but at the time I thought them very clever."[64] These poems were probably "The Fly" and "The Turds of the Scouts" (p. 40). Mrs. Patton may have destroyed the originals, but Patton kept his copies and preserved them even in later years as he was organizing his papers. They survive both in typescript and carbon copies.

Recalling the spirit of Robert Burns' "To a Louse," "The Fly" achieves a kind of mock epic quality when the elevated language of an apostrophe to a "sweet slight friend" is punctured by obscenities and startlingly grotesque images. It is likely that the poem was written to relieve the tedium and to entertain Patton's comrades in Mexico. These included fellow officers, civilian scouts, and a group of war correspondents with whom he was on good terms.]

> O sweet slight friend
> Who frolics free
> O'er cactus plain
> Or sandy lee,
>
> No one can lonely
> Long remain
> While hearkening to
> Thy blithe refrain.

---

64. Blumenson, I, p. 347.

When meal time comes
Thy friendly face
Is everywhere about
The place.

You taste the coffee
Eat oatmeal
And from the cakes the
Syrup steal.

And though we know that
You have been
On the hot turds
In some latrine,

And while you sipped
The dainties there
You gathered germs in
Your long hair,

To spread them
Wantonly upon
Each dainty meat
Or new baked bun.

Still, we can't blame you
For we know
That all we eat
To shit will go.

And after meals
When we would feign
Seek Morpheus[65] arms
From labor pain,

You gently break
Our sweet repose
By deftly fighting[66]
In our nose.

Our ears and mouths
You then explore
And leave there
Pus from some old sore.

Then when at night
You needs must sleep
Onto our tented
Roofs you creep.

---

65. In Greek mythology, Morpheus was the god of dreams.

66. In the carbon copy of this poem at the Library of Congress, "fighting" was originally "fucking." The obscenity has been crossed out and replaced with the less offensive word in a hand that resembles Patton's.

And when the Witching
Hour has come
Your dainty farts
Pervade the gloom,

While like the dews
From heaven fall
Your tiny turds
So round and small.

And if in battle
We should die
Around us first
Would swarm the fly.

You'd do your best
To ease the pain
And swarm around
Each oozing vein.

Yes, in memoria to
A friend
A hundred thousand
Eggs you'd lend.

And as through maggots
Sent by you
Our gruesome corpse
More gruesome grew.

You'd swarm in myriads
Feasting high
You'd hum our dirge
You goddamned fly!

1916

THE TURDS OF THE SCOUTS

[During his Mexican tour of duty, Patton gained a taste of the action he longed for, but overall the assignment was far from the war of his dreams. Pancho Villa's rag-tag guerillas were elusive, denying Patton the opportunity to test – in a cavalry charge – the effectiveness of the new saber he had redesigned and which the army had recently adopted.[67]

---

67. Blumenson, I, pp. 308-309.

The Mexican experience was nonetheless valuable for Patton, in part, because he came into contact with and was enchanted by a new class of people: the roisterous American inhabitants of Texas border towns and ranches. Patton had a genuine affinity for these authentic frontier fighters – mostly gunmen hired by ranch owners for protection against Mexican outlaws – and for their tall tales and raunchy humor.[68]

Two such individuals assigned to the Punitive Expedition as "scouts" were with Patton in the gunfight at the Rubio Ranch. (See "Marching in Mexico," p. 19.) To amuse them and others, he wrote this poem and probably read it aloud with his characteristically florid delivery. In a prose introduction, Patton declared: "It is commonly reported that the scouts attached to the Punitive Expedition are such a tough lot that their turds have gills and breathe and live till evening. Hence this poem."[69] It was at this time that Patton probably began to learn and cultivate the profanity for which he would later become famous.]

> The scout sat in the cactus shade
> He labored mightily
> That he did try to take a shit
> Was very plain to see.
>
> For days and weeks he'd ridden hard
> He'd eaten many a meal
> Yet every morn he waits in vain
> Some bowel movement to feel.
>
> Now scouts by nature are so bad
> That long-imprisoned turds
> Must soon assume their parent's shape
> And too be evil birds.
>
> The faces[70] which in common folk
> Resembles pumpkin pies
> In scouts assumes a texture dark
> Yes, lives and breathes and sighs.

---

68. Blumenson, I, p. 298ff.
69. "The Turds of the Scouts," Patton Papers, Box 60, Library of Congress.
70. Patton was here punning on the word "faeces."

Now as the scout his labor pressed
At last he seemed to feel
A slimy thing crawl from his ass
And purr against his heel.

He little recked, the hardy brute
The suffering he did cause
He did not pause to wipe his ass
He just pulled up his drawers.

He jumped upon his sorebacked horse
And galloped fast away
Oh! little heeded he or cared
What his dying turd would say.

It lay and suffered in the heat
Its limpid eyes rolled high
And from its fast congealing gills
Escaped a gentle sigh.

I came upon it suffering there
I sobbed to see its pain
When the pale green fog my nostrils reached
I held my nose in vain.

I dashed in agony away
My pity turned to pain
And as the sun dipped in the west
It sighed and died amain.

1916

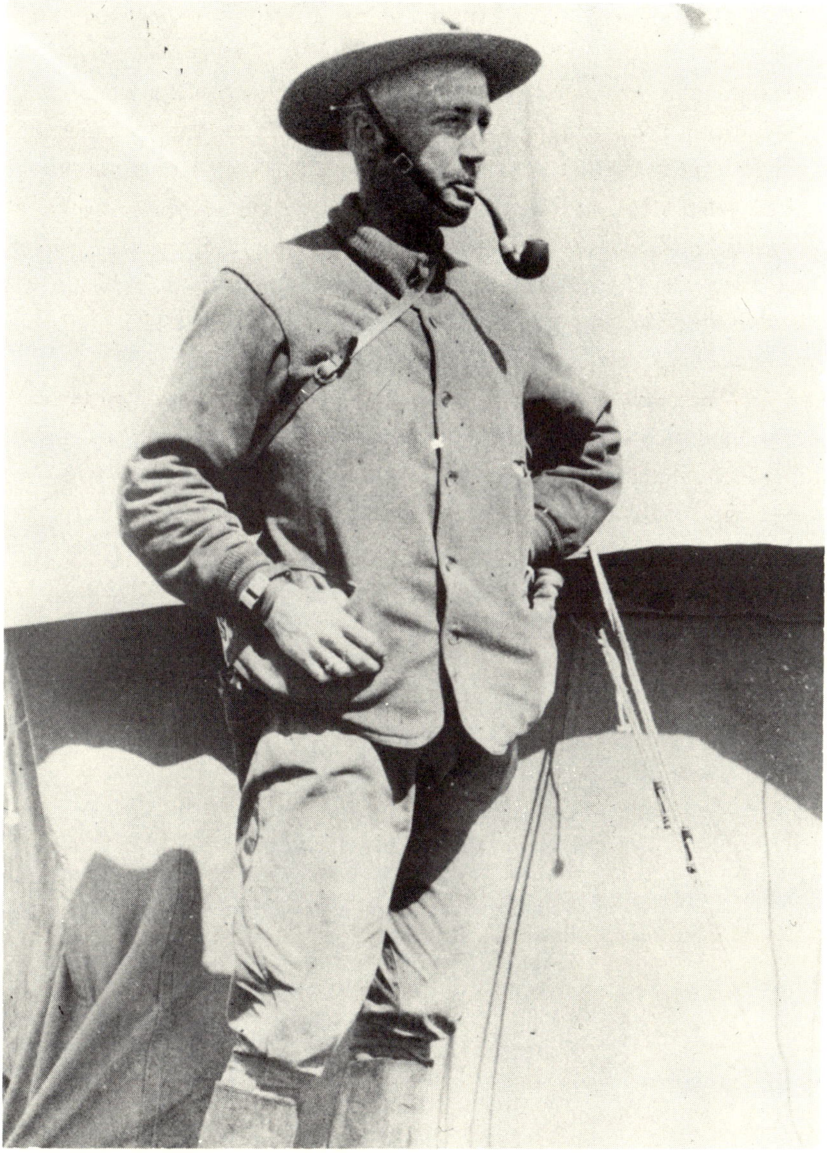

THE ATTACK

[Patton wrote "The Attack" as an attempt "to show fear and its conqueror, Pride."[71] The hero of the poem is a young soldier who faces enemy gunfire and his own death rather than dishonor the "glorious name" of his warrior ancestors whose spirits look on. "The Attack" anticipates a similar experience Patton himself would have two years later amid the shell-pocked battlefields of France. When he was pinned down by German machine guns outside the village of Cheppy, Patton's courage was steeled by the specters of several of his military ancestors beckoning him onward. Rather than risk disgrace in their eyes, he led a reckless attack until he was wounded and could go no further. (See "The Soul in Battle," p. 128.)

The poem is prophetic in another sense. It closes with an invocation to a "God of Battles," the earliest version of the pre-Christian warrior-deity that Patton himself would popularize and come to personify in World War II. (See "God of Battles," p. 141.)]

Death stalked among the combatants
His scythe with blood was dank;
He reaped, with mirthless energy,
From men of every rank.

From noble and from simple,
The hero and the knave,
His ghastly strokes in shrapnel fell
To fill the common grave.

Now, as the lines draw nearer
The level bullets beat,
From hazing mouths of rifles,
Hid in the yellow wheat.

Youths, who at home were pampered,
Pressed forward eagerly,
Vying with callow plow boys,
Which first Death's face should see.

While louder and yet louder
Increased the awful roar,
While acrid in their nostrils rose,
The stink of fresh spilled gore.

---

71. "The Attack," Patton Collection, U. S. Military Academy Library.

And now the trench is entered,
The bayonets thrust home;
From mangled flesh, round prodding points,
Ooze out the guts and foam.

They struggle in that rhapsody,
Which only fighters know;
They club and thrust, while trampling,
Torn friend and writhing foe.

Alas! they stagger backward,
Their valorous dash outworn;
They falter, yet an instant,
In the bullet-winnowed corn.

Fear playing on their heartstrings,
In piteous rout they fly;
Save only one, who turns white faced,
Determined there to die.

It is not courage holds him,
But fear in its mightiest form;
Born of a race of soldiers,
He dares not face their scorn.

His eyes can see Valhalla,
Where staring from the skies
The men who fought for England
Watch how their offspring dies.

And then his vision lengthens,
He sees two eyes of blue,
Soft eyes which seem to worship,
Trusting his courage true.

No longer now he falters,
Can man betray such love?
Deserted by his fellows,
His strength comes from above.

He staggers towards the rifles,
He crumples in their flame,
He falls another victim,
But saves a glorious name.

Shame on faint hearts that babble
Of justice and of right,
Yet speak of war as murder
And deride the men who fight.

'Tis only battle raised men
To noblest sacrifice,
And war alone can purge our hearts
Of cowardice and vice.

Speak not of those who perish
As lives wasted in vain;
No more than mother's labour
Has been for naught their pain.

To each of us in peace and war
There comes a time to go;
To each one's friends at such a time
There comes the loss and woe.

But is it not far better
To die one's land to save,
Than having lived in slothful peace
To sink to nameless grave?

Which one of us by peaceful death
Can leave to heirs to come,
The pride which conquers cowardice
To save noble name?

Oh! Glorious God of Battle,
Preserve to us the race,
Of those who scorning worldly gain
Fear death less than disgrace.

Let not our growing affluence
Make us unfit to fight;
But make us eager, now as e'er
To keep our honor bright.

1916

THE VISION

[The simple truth related to carrying out what Patton often called "the oldest of honorable professions"[72] was that to be a soldier a man must be ready to kill his fellow man. Philosophically, at least, Patton distanced himself from the enemy to the extent that he could take human life dispassionately and impersonally. While the actual killing of a respected foe was something Patton understood in mythic terms as a sacred event, a blood consecration of the warrior brotherhood, the prospect of his own death loomed as an almost tantalizing affirmation of his warrior status. Over and over again, as a wartime officer and peacetime polo player, Patton exhibited

---

72. Lecture, "The Obligation of Being an Officer," October 1, 1919, Blumenson, I, p. 723.

II

1917-1918

WORLD WAR I

And now again I am here for war
Where as Roman and knight I have been
Again I practice to fight the Hun
And attack him by machine.

>"Memories Roused by a Roman Theater"
>Captain George S. Patton, Jr.

a recklessness that appeared suicidal. But the General's attraction toward death also found important expression in his poetry.

Toward the end of his assignment with the Punitive Expedition, Patton wrote "The Vision" and "The Bronco Pass" (p. 48). While these poems reveal a kind of gloating enthusiasm for blood and gore, they are also serious mental exercises evoking images of violent death, Patton's own and that of "a poor goddamned recruit." In effect, he used his imagination to supply in poetry the experience he sought – vainly, so far – in combat.

Apart from the fifteen-minute gunfight at the Rubio Ranch, Patton had not encountered military action of the sort he renders here, but he would not have long to wait. On April 6, 1917, President Wilson signed the congressional resolution declaring war against Germany, and, in May, General Pershing was appointed to lead the American Expeditionary Force to France. As luck, charm and personal contacts would have it, Patton was assigned to his staff. They arrived in Liverpool with an advance party of American soldiers on June 8, and, to Patton's great relief, were in France within earshot of the big guns less than a week later.]

>Fiercely the squadron followed
>Trampling the withered grass
>And I heard the clatter as men went down
>And the hiss of the shots that pass.
>
>And then one came before its sound[73]
>I fell for an endless way
>Till a mighty calm engulfed me
>And I woke to a clearer day.
>
>The dust no longer choked me
>The charge seethed far ahead
>A limp form lay beneath my mare
>Its face was mine and – dead.

---

73. A reference to the idea that, since a bullet travels faster than the speed of sound, its victim will fall or be rendered unconscious before he hears the shot.

I looked at the thing which I had been
The blood oozed from its face
At the sword[74] I had known so well to use
Now limp in death's embrace.

I thought complacently of fame
And how I had broken the foe
But then I thought with gripping pain
Of those I loved – their woe.

As I mused, the miles had vanished
I stood in my childhood's home
While she I loved stood near me
Yet knew not I had come.

I saw the smile upon her lips
While the flowers bloomed beside
I could not bear that she should hear
That I had really died.

My thirst for glory faded then
Before unselfish love
I prayed to live for her – not fame.
They say my stunned mare moved...

Her struggles caught a searcher's eye
They carried me away
And when I woke days later
'Twas near my love I lay.

1917

THE BRONCO PASS

We crouched on the rocky hilltop,
The key to the Bronco Pass;
While the heat waves rose up, wiggling
Where the wounded lay in the grass.

They lay there in the blistering heat
Of early afternoon;
We couldn't even quench their thirst,
For all our water was gone.

---

74. Details such as the sword and, in the previous stanza, the mare, indicate that the speaker of this poem is an officer, probably Patton himself, who was a well-known horseman and, in 1914, was the U. S. Army's first Master of the Sword.

The dark blood dried in tricklets.
From punctured bellies came
Bubbles, the stinkingness of which
Has never found a name.

Yet still we held to the boulders,
Hoping supports would come;
And still, on every side of us,
Crawled ever closer – doom.

The grit from smitten granite
Flew blinding in our eyes;
The bullets, screaming overhead
Drowned out our wounded's cries.

Now, only five of us were left
And three of them were hit;
Yet still we fought, despairing,
Like trapped rats in a pit.

The man beside me shuddered,
His brains shut out my sight.
I tried to wipe the goo away,
And when I woke 'twas night.

You say they found me when they came,
Laying amongst the dead;
Hugging my empty rifle
With a bullet in my head?

No I haven't any parents
And I haven't any folks;
I'm just a poor goddamned recruit,
And this is where I croaks.

The soldier ceased from speaking,
The room was very still;
The doctor, stooping, closed the eyes
Of him who held the hill.

1917

Tanks of the 304th American Tank Brigade, commanded by Patton, move into action in the Meuse-Argonne campaign in September 1918.

U.S. Army photo
Courtesy of the Patton Museum

MUD

[In June 1917, Patton was where he most wanted to be: near the European war and attached to the headquarters of General Pershing. It would still be more than a year before he went into action, but at least the possibility of combat was now within sight. On June 24, he wrote that none of Pershing's staff had yet observed any fighting, and for the next several weeks he encouraged his wife to come to France, which Patton described as "just like a great lawn."[1] On July 20, Pershing and a half-dozen officers, including Patton, visited the headquarters of Field Marshall Sir Douglas Haig at Mons-en-Peule, where they were regaled with guards of honor and where they discussed the organization of American troops who would soon be pouring into France.

Upon his return from Haig's headquarters, Patton wrote "Mud," a poem at once shocking and jovial in its songlike description of the human debris of war. For all of the poem's grisly details, however, nothing in Patton's otherwise candid letters and diary indicates his familiarity at this time with the corpse-strewn fields of France and Belgium. It is likely that he

---

1. Blumenson, I, p. 404. In the summer of 1917, Patton could still describe wartime France as a "great lawn" because, as a member of Pershing's staff, he would have been stationed far behind the front lines. His comment indicates the degree to which General Headquarters staff were insulated from the realities of trench warfare. In 1916, for example, Field Marshal Haig's chief of intelligence described the administrative difficulties and discouragements high-level officers experienced when they ventured toward the front. He wrote that there were "few visible signs of war" at General Headquarters, and added: "We might almost be in England." Quoted in John Keegan, *The Mask of Command* (New York: Viking Penguin, 1987), pp. 333-34.

was provided with such details by his friend, Captain John G. Quekmeyer, one of a small number of American officers who had been to the front.[2]

Patton devoted his life to the principles of martial courage and self-sacrifice, so what do we make of a poem that appears to mock the putrefying flesh of fallen soldiers, that dehumanizes their remains as "bloody offal"? It is clear that "Mud," like "The Fly" written during the previous year (p. 38), are darkly ironic responses to war's atrocities. They are grisly expressions of a kind of gallows humor shared by those for whom fighting, killing and the prospect of dying violently are daily realities. In his World War I memoir, for example, Coningsby Dawson, a Canadian artillery observer, recalled one of the "many mad burlesques" sung (to the tune of "A Little Bit of Heaven") by front-line soldiers:

> Oh, a little bit of shrapnel fell
>   from out the sky one day,
> And it landed on a soldier
>   in a field not far away;
> But when they went to find him
>   he was bust beyond repair,
> So they pulled his legs and arms off
>   and they left him lying there.
>
> Then they buried him in Flanders
>   just to make the new crop grow.
> He'll make the best manure, they say,
>   and sure they ought to know.
> And they put a little cross up
>   which bore his name so grand,
> On the day he took his farewell
>   for a better Promised Land.

"One learns to laugh – one has to – " Dawson wrote," just as one has to learn to believe in immortality."[3]]

---

2. Blumenson, I, p. 402.

3. Coningsby Dawson, *The Glory of the Trenches* (New York: John Lane, 1918), pp. 124-25.

Oh! the Tommies and Poilu in the mud,[4]
Oh! the Belgians and the Sammies[5] in the mud,
Bloody mud, made with blood,
Where they die.

Oh! the humming of the gothas[6] overhead,
And the squeaking of the rats who gnaw our dead,
In the mud, black with blood,
Where they lie.

Oh! the thudding of bomb fragments into flesh,
And the gurgling of the wounded as they splash,
In the trampled, bloody mud,
Where they sink.

Oh! the howling and the crashing of the shells,
Wicked things, devilish things, hellish elves,
Ough! the swelling of the bodies in the mud,
Where they stink.

So we drag 'em from the trenches in the end,
Bloody offal[7] that was once, perhaps, a friend,
And we chuck 'em in a shell hole full of blood,
Jesus help 'em! They are rotten in the mud.

1917

---

4. The French summer of 1917 was an especially wet one. In his Diary for July 29 Patton recorded: "Heavy rain and hail storm. Very hot in afternoon." Patton Papers, Box 1, Library of Congress.

5. "Tommies," "Poilu" and "Sammies" were colloquial terms for World War I British, French and American soldiers.

6. "Gothas" were German twin-engine bombers. Each airplane carried six 110-pound fragmentation bombs.

7. The image here refers to the mutilated remains of soldiers killed by artillery shells. It is also, however, a pun on the British expression "bloody awful," which Patton had written in the original text. When he later edited the poem for possible publication, he apparently could not resist the pun and wrote "offal" over the word "awful."

DUSK

["Dusk" and "The Air Raid" (p. 57) provide a glimpse of the subtlety Patton was capable of when he put his mind to it. Because "The Air Raid" was probably written several years after "Dusk," we can observe a poetically more mature writer at work, developing an idea and honing his imagery, making it at once sharper and more evocative. The "shrouded windows" in "Dusk," for example, become the even more ominous "ill-shrouded windows" in "The Air Raid." Similarly, the line"...high in the *blue* of the lipwarm sky" becomes "High in the *heart* of the lip-warm sky." In both poems, the reference to the sound of the descending bombs is soothingly hypnotic, indeed almost maternal, as they "hum" toward their targets. Both poems recreate a tranquil atmosphere about to be shattered by the instruments of war; but while "Dusk" brings us only to the edge of the crisis, "The Air Raid" takes us through the crisis and, finally, to its ghastly after-effects. In the later poem, the "holy calm" is shattered and then restored, but with a deathly difference: the "flitting shadows" of the opening stanza become the "burial parties" of the last.]

    Dusk and the soldiers wander
    At ease in the village street
    Done with sweat and drilling
    Was ever rest more sweet?

    Night and from shrouded windows
    The careless lamplights glow
    When high in the blue of the lipwarm sky
    Comes the double hum[8] we know.

1917?

---

8. The "double hum" refers to the drone of the twin-engine "Gothas." (See also "Mud," p. 53.)

THE AIR RAID

Along the still and muddied street,
The flitting shadows go,
Athwart the ghastly beams of light,
Ill-shrouded windows throw.

While hill and valley, town and farm,
In Sabbath stillness bound,
Where the far guns' incessant boom
Makes silence more than sound.

High in the heart of the lip-warm sky
Sounds the double hum of the foe,
And the holy calm of the village farm
Is split with a crash and glow.

From front and rear, from far and near,
The cackling Hotchkiss[9] speak,
While tracer bullets and star shells light
The clouds, where the shrapnels seek.

Along the hum of the muddied street,
The burial parties go,
Athwart the ghastly beams of light,
Ill-shrouded windows throw.

1921

THE TRENCH RAID

[Although it was not his ideal of combat (the cavalry charge was more his style), Patton would have led a clandestine nighttime raid into enemy lines if he had been given the opportunity. He could hardly have hoped for such a mission as a member of General Pershing's staff, but later as a tank commander Patton would demonstrate courage during close combat. Until then, he more or less contented himself with poetic re-creations of the kind of fighting that he fancied was taking place. In poems like "The Trench Raid," Patton gave free reign to his pent-up imagination. At times, as in the onomatopoeic description of the "rush and trip and slithering rip" of the

---

9. A machine gun used by U. S. troops during World War I.

bayonet, the results were as gruesome as they are unforgettable. Mrs. Patton liked this poem, calling it "one of the best."[10]]

> In the awesome hush of midnight
> 'Neath the leering light of the stars
> There past the shattered poplars
> The raiding party stirs.
>
> Slowly, with infinite caution
> Creeping and prowling they go
> Slinking in cratered shadows
> Stooping by gaps, bent low.
>
> Stopping to peer and listen
> Tripping on putrid dead
> Halting in haggard expectance
> When the flare burns overhead.
>
> Onward, like evil pixies
> Nearer and nearer the foe
> Hoping he will not hear them
> Dreading the unseen blow.
>
> Out of the dark a challenge
> Into the dark a bomb
> Then the rush and trip and slithering rip
> As the bayonet thrusts go home.
>
> In the lurid light of the barrage
> 'Neath the whine and whoop of the shell
> Past the clear black line of the poplars
> Come the raiders, back from Hell.

1917?

THE SONG OF THE EMBUSQUÉ

["Embusqué" is French military slang for "slacker" or "goldbricker," a soldier on a special assignment not requiring participation in the usual training and fatigue details.[11] (See also "The Slacker," p. 71.) Such was hardly the duty Patton desired, but weeks had passed since his arrival in

---

10. "The Trench Raid," Patton Collection, U. S. Military Academy Library.

11. John. R. Elting, Dan Cragg and Ernest L. Deal, *A Dictionary of Soldier Talk* (New York: Scribner's, 1984), s.v. "goldbrick."

France and he had yet to see or do any real fighting. By August 1917, he channeled his frustration into irony and formed what he called an exclusive "club." "To be a member," he wrote to Beatrice, "you must be a cavalry man who never rides and who never goes within fourteen miles of the trenches."[12] Known as the "Embusqué," the club had three members, each of whom is mentioned in the "song" that Patton wrote: Captain Carl Boyd, Captain John G. Quekmeyer and Patton himself, who "writes bum verse for which he will swing."[13]]

> I sing the song of the Embusqué
> Those who always home do stay
> And never far from Paris stray
> Ho! for the jolly Embusqué.
>
> I sing in praise of our President
> Captain Boyd with legs so bent
> Who never will go nor yet be sent
> To the trenches where so many have went.
>
> I sing in honor of dear old Quek
> Who went to Europe and never came back
> For cavalry spirit we never shall lack
> While we look at the legs and ass of Quek.
>
> And last of the member I needs must sing
> Who has never as yet done a useful thing
> But who still hangs onto an easy thing
> And writes bum verse for which he will swing.
>
> Then here's HOW to the jolly Embusqué
> May they live right on to Judgement Day
> And never far from Paris stray
> Salute, Salute to the Embusqué.

1917

---

12. Letter to "Beatrice," August 17, 1917, Blumenson, I, p. 412.

13. Both of Patton's friends later died of pneumonia, Boyd in February 1919, Quekmeyer early in 1926, just after his selection as Commandant of the U. S. Military Academy. Blumenson, I, pp. 684, 800.

RUBBER SHOES

[To the envy of all of his fellow officers and even many of his superiors who were far less wealthy than he, Patton enjoyed the luxury of possessing his own automobile while stationed in Europe. Despite the intensity of German submarine attacks upon Allied shipping, his Packard five-seater arrived safely in France shortly after he did. Some time later, Patton came upon a pair of his wife's rubber shoes that were stowed away in the car. Mrs. Patton's daughter, Ruth Ellen, remembered Patton telling her mother that the galoshes were too big: "When she had them on she walked like a duck."[14]]

While searching in my motor car
To get a can of grease
I came upon some rubber shoes
The shoes of Beatrice.

You who have never met her
Of course can hardly know
The train of deep emotions
Those rubbers set aglow.

For gazing on them brought to mind
The picture of her feet
And dainty legs in stockings trim
Duckwalking up the street.

The memory of her cunningness
And of her crooked tooth
The tragic thought that far from her
I'd passed the half our youth.

So picking up the grease can
I sadly turned aside
And jammed a hub cap full of goo
My woeful thoughts to hide.

1917

---

14. Letter, Ruth Ellen Patton Totten to Carmine A. Prioli, June 25, 1988.

A CODE OF ACTION

[Patton wrote this poem and sent it to Beatrice on December 20, 1917. He was in the French town of Langres attempting to establish a light tank training center. Since tank warfare was in its infancy, the assignment gave Patton the opportunity to accomplish something more or less on his own. The British and French armored forces had already demonstrated that tanks could be effective in combat, but many theoretical and logistical problems still had to be solved. So Patton's assignment was professionally a risky one, and he was dispirited by the fact that it was taking an unexpectedly long time to actually acquire tanks and get the training underway.

Consequently, Patton wrote this poem, he said, "to inspire myself."[15] It was, in part, Patton's poetic response to the idea that he was destined for greatness, and even apparently inauspicious assignments would lead to unforeseen triumphs. Although World War I would end too soon to bear out Patton's prediction, World War II would later validate his remarkable prescience. On March 13, 1943, for example, the day following Patton's promotion to Lieutenant General, he had been reading poetry and came upon what he called "a great line":

>I didn't begin with askings
>I took my job and stuck
>I took the chances they wouldn't
>And now they are calling it luck.[16]]

>In wondrous catlike ability
>For grasping all things which go by
>To land on my feet with agility
>No one is greater than I.

>In doing the things others will not
>In standing the blows others shirk
>In grasping the chance that returns not
>And never yet shirking my work.

---

15. "A Code of Action," Patton Papers, Box 60, Library of Congress.

16. "Diary," March 13, 1943, Box 3, Patton Papers, Library of Congress. Patton noted that the lines were from "The *Mary Gloster*," a poem by Kipling.

>For these gifts, Oh! God, I thank Thee
>Pray let me continue the same
>Since, by doing things well which are nearest
>Perhaps I shall yet rise to fame.
>
>It is not in intricate planning
>Nor yet in regretting the past
>That great men whose lives we are watching
>Have gained to their greatness at last.
>
>Hence praise we the just mead of striving
>Which foolish make light of as luck
>There never was yet luck in shirking
>While much is accomplished through pluck.
>
>So seize I the things which are nearest
>And studious fall on my feet
>Do ever in all things my damndest
>And never, Oh, never retreat!
>
>   1917

THE END OF WAR

[At the end of this poem, which was written on December 30, 1917, Patton noted that it was "an attempt to express my prevailing idea in verse. I had the notion for over a year but the result is not up to the effort."[17] The "prevailing idea" is that war will not end, despite the evolutionary progress of man. In fact, Patton believed that war was a necessary prerequisite for civilization. He was, no doubt, responding to those who spoke of the European conflict as the war to end all wars. Such an idea was altogether wrongheaded to Patton, who saw truth in the martial philosophy of German General Friedrich von Bernhardi and others. "History," Bernhardi wrote in 1912, "shows that war is a powerful instrument of civilization....As wars were necessary for human progress in the past, we may conclude that they will also be necessary to progress in the future."[18]]

---

17. "The End of War," Patton Papers, Box 60, Library of Congress.

18. Friedrich von Bernhardi, *Britain as Germany's Vassal*, p. 111.

When the hairy apes of long ago
Battled for days to see
Whether the tails of future apes
Should straight or curly be,

Other apes whose hair more sparsely grew
And the shes who were great with child
Hung from branches up side down
And sighed, and gibbered, and smiled,

They said: "Such sights are hardly nice
"For tails are what they are.
"'Tis savage and like the wolves,
"This must be the end of war."

When the painted savages of the swamps
Slew the clay-daubed men of the brae
In order to settle by flint and club
Which clan might draw mammoths on clay,

The craven lake-folk, smeared with fat,
Crouched on their rafts and said:
"Though insects bite us through our grease
"'Tis better than being dead."

"Our cultured smell makes us despised
"We live a mildewed life
"But we are the people of brotherly love.
"This *must* be the end of strife."

The gentle Persian fled before
The warlike men of Greece;
The phalanx broke their masses
So they advocated peace.[19]

They praised the purple coated fop
Whose hands were white and slim;
They loathed the sweaty brute in bronze
And, loathing, fled from him.

While huddled in their harlots' arms
Their land in flames they saw;
Yet kissed the painted odalisques[20]
And cried: "'Tis the end of war."

---

19. The reference is to Alexander the Great's invasion of Asia Minor and his defeat of the Persian Empire in 334 B. C.

20. A harem slave or concubine.

When Carthage conquered far off Spain
And all but conquered Rome
She suffered from the lethargy
Of fighting far from home.

She deified domestic quiet
Her youth would no more fight
Till bloody Zama's[21] fatal day
Destroyed for e'er her might.

For having conquered Spain she thought
Like countless fools before
That having gained her peace by strife
There would be no more war.

'Twere idle further to recount
The folly of mankind
Who gaining all by battle
To future wars grows blind.

The folly of the slogan
Down all the ages rings
The ruin of republics
The funeral dirge of kings.

"At last the strife is ended;
"Battles shall rage no more;
"The time of perfect peace has come;
"There *can* be no more war."

Still, like the foolish revelers
In Babylon's banquet hall
They'll take their ease while mocking
The writing on the wall.

They will disband their armies
When this great strife[22] is won,
And trust again to pacifists
To guard for them their home.

They will return to futileness
As quickly as before
Though Truth and History vainly shout
"THERE IS NO END TO WAR."

1917

---

21. Zama, an ancient town in North Africa, was the scene of the defeat of the Carthaginians under Hannibal by the Romans under Scipio Africanus in 202 B. C.

22. "This great strife" refers to World War I.

MEMORIES ROUSED BY A ROMAN THEATER

[Late in 1917, Patton was an observer at the tank training school for French officers at Chamlieu. For two weeks, he learned all he could about the development and operations of tank warfare. At the end of his brief tour, Patton wrote a report that became the "rock upon which the American tank effort was established."[23] During this time, he also toured the walled town of Langres and wrote this poem, which combines his belief in reincarnation with his newfound destiny as a tank commander. Patton romanticized the armored, mechanized vehicle as the modern example of earlier forms of armor, the "brass of Rome" and the "rattling plate" of medieval knights astride their restless chargers.[24]

Among the various "ruins of Rome" at Langres, Patton – the amateur archaeologist – ascertained that a Roman gate was still part of the city's walls and that drawbridges of Roman vintage were still operable.[25]]

I sat in my throbbing *Char d'Assaut*[26]
In the shade of the ruins of Rome,
And I knew that despite the dimming years
This place had once been home.

Yes, more than once have I seen these walls
Rise sharp on the brow of the hill;
And more than once have I trod that road
That winds like a snake from the rill.

---

23. Blumenson, I, p. 448.

24. In a lecture he delivered in 1928 entitled "Tanks, Past and Future," Patton said: "Forerunners of the modern tank...were the Trojan horse conceived by Laertes' godlike son Ulysses, which was itself the forerunner of the movable towers used by Alexander against Tyre, and certain engines called the Sow, the Bore, and the Cat, which were intended for siege warfare in antiquity and medieval times." Blumenson, I, p. 835.

25. Blumenson, I, p. 439.

26. "*Char d'Assaut*" (assault car) was a French two-man miniature tank designed by Louis Renault and improved upon by American manufacturers.

First it was in the brass of Rome
With the white dust on my brow;
And the second time 'neath the flag of a Duke
Whose name is legend now.

And that old rock so chipped and worn
Was a bench in an earlier day;
And I rested on it while hurrying slaves
Stripped helm and greaves[27] away.

This hollow where the three small arches are
Was a pool of water clear,
Which mirrored the forms of war scarred men
Who bathed and rested here.

Later I passed in rattling plate
When time had crumbled the walls;
And a laurel thicket covered the slopes
That once were watchers' stalls.

'Twas here they brought us after the fight
We had in the field out there;
And underneath that pile of stones
Is the place where our corpses are.

And now again I am here for war
Where as Roman and knight I have been;
Again I practice to fight the Hun
And attack him by machine.

So the three old hags[28] still play their game;
Still men the counters are;
And many peg out in the game of peace;
Pray God my count shall be war!

1917

---

27. "Helm and greaves" are head and shin protectors.

28. The "three old hags" are the Fates. In Greek mythology, they were the three goddesses who controlled human destiny: the first (Clotho) spun the thread of life, the second (Lachesis) determined its length, and the third (Atropos) cut it off.

Lt. Col. Patton in France during the summer of 1918, standing in front of a Renault tank, one of his "precious babies."
U.S. Army photo
Courtesy of the Patton Museum

THE PRECIOUS BABIES

[During World War I, Patton specialized in the 6.5-ton light tanks that spluttered and stalled in the mudfields of France and Belgium. They were "babies" in relation to their much larger counterparts, the Mark VIIIs, which carried eleven-men crews and weighed 43.5 tons. But Patton's reference to the light tanks as babies is appropriate in another sense. Shortly after the war, he said: "Only those of us who doctored and nursed the grotesque war babies of 1918 through the innumerable inherent ills of premature birth know how bad they really were,..."[29] Later, in 1918, he wrote: "The 'Baby Tank,' as the French affectionately called the little Renault, was an infant in more respects than size...all the faults of adolescence; feeble, clumsy and nearsighted, it only survived due to the indomitable will of the men who fought and tended it...."[30]

Although the Renaults were dangerous to operate and were of limited effectiveness, Patton nevertheless saw great potential in their combination of armor, mobility and firepower, and because they were theoretically compatible with his own aggressive style of fighting. In his 1917 application for assignment to the newly formed Tank Service, Patton outlined his sentiments and his special qualifications:

> I have always believed in getting close to the enemy and...I believe that I am the only American who has ever made an attack in a motor vehicle. [See "Marching in Mexico," p. 19.] This request is not made because I dislike my present duty or am desirous of evading it, but because I believe when we get 'Tanks' I would be able to do good service in them.[31]

Few of Patton's statements would prove to be as prophetic as this one. During World War I, he went on to establish the U. S. Army's Tank Corps and, in 1943, would train another, vastly more numerous and powerful generation of American tankers in the science of armored warfare.]

---

29. Lecture, "The History, Employment and Tactics of Light Tanks," September 1919, Blumenson, I, p. 719.

30. Untitled article (1919), Blumenson, I, p. 865.

31. Blumenson, I, p. 427.

Up and down the roadways,
    Through the German ranks,
Nosing out machine guns,
    Come the baby tanks.
Scrambling through the crater,
    Splashing through the pool,
Like the Usher's[32] happy boys,
    Bounding out of school.

Fritz is great on wirefields,
    Trust the Boche for that,
But his choicest efforts
    Fall extremely flat.
Wasted in the weaving
    Of laborious days,
When the merry infant class
    Scampers through the maze.

Cheerful little children
    Of an American brain,[33]
Winning ravished country
    Back to France again.
On thru town and village
    Shepherded by Yanks
Romping, blithe and rollicking,
    Roll the baby tanks.

1918

THE SONG OF THE TURDS OF LANGRES

[While organizing the American Light Tank Center and School, Patton had time on his hands as he awaited the arrival of his tanks from the United States. "The Song of the Turds of Langres" is one of several poems, possibly a drinking song, he wrote during this period. Although this poem is not among those Patton intended to publish, the Preface he wrote for that volume includes comments that shed some light on what he called "rough" talk. "Like other diseases of childhood," he wrote, "[it] is but transitory and the fact that it is the common parlance of heroes in no way detracts from the

---

32. An obsolete British term referring to an assistant teacher.

33. The "American brain" is probably a reference to Patton himself, who devised many modifications for the Renault tank.

splendor of their deeds. It is the language of a period, not a profession."[34] Transitory or not, Patton continued to use vulgarity in highly imaginative ways throughout his military career.]

Dedicated to "Warren Lott"[35]

Hark to the song of the turds of Langres
Whose black and gruesome shapes
Which litter up the sidewalks
And slither 'neath our steps.

The turds which in America
Old Warren Lott has seen
To him appeared less brutish
And look less fierce and mean.

'Tis his opinion, we fear,
On shittings he has seen
That such turds are not shit at all
But broken off quite clean.

Lott has a project cherished
To gather all these turds
And shoot them off as solid shot
To slay the Hunish herds.

But Tate[36] avers 'twere better far
To grease the shit with cheese
So that these shots will deadlier grow
And gas the Boche with ease.

'Tis my opinion we could find
Cheese in sufficient lots
If we would simply strain the piss
We find in French piss pots.

So this is the song of the turds of Langres
Whose texture is so tough
That when they fall on sidewalks
The hard stones cry "Enough!"

1918

---

34. "Preface," Patton Papers, Box 60, Library of Congress. Also Blumenson, I, p. 722.

35. A pun on "warring lot."

36. A fellow officer and longtime friend of Patton.

THE SLACKER

[In his popular World War I classic, *Over the Top*, Arthur Guy Empey defined a "slacker" as "An insect in England who is afraid to join the Army. There are three things in this world that Tommy [the British soldier] hates," wrote Empey in his humorous "so-called dictionary" of the trenches: "a slacker, a German, and a trench-rat; it's hard to tell which he hates worst."[37]

"The Slacker" is Patton's poetic contribution to the literature attacking those who would shirk their military responsibilities. It was written on January 17, 1918, when Patton was thirty-two years old. The line describing those who "are under thirty-one and have their health" is probably a reference to the eighteen officers who had just been assigned to his tank school. Since his days at West Point, Patton had a fearsome reputation for requiring nearly impossible perfection from his subordinates.[38] He demanded the highest standards from himself and he therefore had the utmost contempt for those whose performance in the line of duty was indifferent or wanting. "The Slacker" seems to have been an after-hours accompaniment to Patton's routine lectures on discipline and duty. (See also "The Song of the Embusqué," p. 58.) It is uncertain how effective the poem was as satire, but not even the dullest of Patton's new cadre could have failed to get the message.]

> What's this creature now appearing
> Virtue scoffing, manhood jeering
> Whose only motive is to save its skin?

---

37. Arthur Guy Empey, *Over the Top* (New York & London: Putnam's, 1917), p. 308.

38. At West Point, Patton's reputation for disciplining Plebes resulted in a demotion for him as well as the nickname "Quill Georgie." See *The Howitzer* (1907), which defines "quill" as the "excessive skinning of underclassmen."

It is neither man nor woman
Yet 'tis more of brute than human.
It's a Slacker and the worst there is is said.

Such are they that save the nation
Giving lectures on the ration
Yet are under thirty-one and have their health.
Such an one though clothed in ermine
Is far viler than are vermin.
He's a Slacker and the worst there is is said.

You who suffer them and scoff not
Aid to damn the land with dry rot
Their example is a menace to the race.
You should drive them from their places
Spit their lies into their faces.
They are Slackers and 'twere better
    they were dead.

They are myriad, these abortions
With their shirking, stinking notions
False to manhood, false to country, false to God
They are neither men nor women
They are more of curs than human
They are Slackers, may God damn them
    till they're dead.

1918

TO YOUR PICTURE

[Patton wrote this poem on June 25, 1918, after receiving a photograph of his wife. At around the same time, he noted that four of his officers had been arrested for drinking publicly with French women. Although Patton did not think highly of such fraternization, he had no deep-seated objections to it. "People who are going to be killed," he wrote, "deserve as much pleasure as they can get." He declared to Beatrice that he was not "one of these pleasure seekers,"[39] and may have included the following poem as further assurance.]

---

39. Blumenson, I, p. 548.

Your picture here before me shows too well,
The sweetness which I know is latent there,
The pleading torment of your laughing eyes,
The maddening rapture of your glorious hair.

Shown without color, flat, and without breath,
Your subtle charm yet gives the picture life,
And makes the cardboard throb and thrill again,
With those dear passions which are yours, my wife.

Though distance parts us with the heaving sea,
And time essays to dull your face and form,
The last is impotent to blind my eyes,
And your dear face shines clearer through the storm.

Though I have naught of you but thoughts to cheer,
Your spirit aids me in the throbbing strife,
And aught I do, I do for you alone,
You, my one love, my body and my life.

1918

YOU NEVER CAN TELL ABOUT A WOMAN

[Martin Blumenson notes that Patton sent this lyric, exemplifying "charm and humor," to a senior member of Pershing's headquarters in 1918.[40]]

You never can tell about a woman,
Perhaps that's why you think they are so nice;
You never see two alike at any one time,
And you never see one alike twice.

You are never very certain that they love you,
You are often very certain that they don't;
For a man may argue still that he has the strongest will,
But a woman has the strongest won't.

1918

---

40. Blumenson, II, p. 856.

RECOLLECTIONS – A. E. F.[41]

[For all of the profound seriousness with which Patton approached his career and what he called his "destiny," he could still laugh at himself, often privately in his letters and somewhat more publicly in his humorous verses. Undoubtedly, the most hilarious image of all is the one in this Kiplingesque poem of young "Blood 'n Guts," the doughty commander of American tanks, straddling a bidet.]

When this cruel war is over
    and we've laid aside our hates
When we've crossed the bounding billow
    to our loved United States
When I sleep in real pajamas,
    not in sweater, sock and pants
I will think about the billet
    where I froze in sunny France.

When I sit all snug and cozy
    and it isn't any dream
That I hear the radiator hissing
    merrily with steam
When the house is warm and comfy,
    here's an idea I advance
I'll forgive the heating systems
    that are all the vogue in France.

When I watch an open fire
    eating up the seasoned logs
I'll recall the sappy sticks fresh cut
    from slimy Gallic bogs
When I hear the fire crackle,
    when I watch it jump and dance
I'll forget the smoking fireplace
    I froze beside in France.

When I get up in the morning
    from a decent Christian bed
And my teeth no longer chatter
    till they loosen in my head
When I choose twixt the tub and the shower,
    then there really is a chance
That I'll laugh about the lady's bath
    I straddled back in France.

---

41. "A.E.F." was the abbreviation for American Expeditionary Force, the Yankee counterpart to the B. E. F., the British Expeditionary Force.

I'll go into my toilet room
    and find it always neat
Warm and odorless and clean
    with a polished oaken seat
Where the pipes are never frozen,
    then this budding poet grants
He will shiver when he thinks
    about the icy cans in France.

I'll slip into my bed at night
    beneath a quilted spread
That'll tuck in at the bottom,
    while it covers up my head
Whether lovely woman shares it,
    or I sleep alone perchance
I'll never miss the liver pad[42]
    I froze beneath in France.

Every morning when I'm shaving
    and the running water steams
I'll think of freezing shaves abroad
    as odd fantastic dreams
But when I see a chamber pot
    there isn't any chance
I'll forget the mug of amber ice
    beneath my bed in France.

1918

MERCENARY'S SONG (A. D. 1600)

[On April 17, 1918, Patton received medical treatment for a skin problem. While in a camp hospital, he wrote "Mercenary's Song (A. D. 1600)" to "amuse a Red Cross nurse."[43] In a simple transcription of the poem, the humor is quite lost. One has to imagine the inflection, nuance and gesture that Patton, a natural performer, would have used to provide the comic element that is altogether missing in the poem's printed form.

---

42. A "liver pad" or "liver patch" was army slang for the General Staff Identification Patch, so called because it was worn on the uniform blouse above the wearer's liver. There may also be a reference here to the liver pads sold by medical quacks to prevent the user from getting an unexpected chill. See Elting, *A Dictionary of Soldier Talk*, s.v. "liver pad."

43. "Mercenary's Song," Patton Papers, Box 60, Library of Congress.

That "Mercenary's Song" was intended to be more mischievous than bloodcurdling is suggested by the fact that Patton later taught it to his youngest daughter, Ruth Ellen, who was then instructed to recite it for her schoolmaster. He was a man for whom neither she nor her father had much regard, but they apparently enjoyed shaking him up. The General also taught his three children to curse "wickedly," but in lines from Shakespeare. That way, they could get away with it, and few of their classmates – and teachers – would be much the wiser.[44]

Patton sent copies of "Mercenary's Song" and the far more serious "Soldier's Religion" to Beatrice, asking for her opinion and saying, "Please don't throw them away."[45]]

> I am no callow Christian
> No pus-paunched prelate I
> I dream not of salvation
> Nor fear the day I'll die.
>
> In wantonness of appetite
> In women, wine, and war
> In strife and blood and rapine
> In these my pleasures are.
>
> I love the smell of horse dung
> The sight of corpse-strewn mud
> The sound of steel on armour
> The feel of clotting blood.
>
> The women I have ravished
> The infants I have slain
> The priests and nuns I've roasted
> They haunt me not again.
>
> Priests talk of souls' salvation
> And shining lights afar
> But give me women's laughter
> And the battle flash of war.
>
> Priests talk of souls' damnation
> And the white hot pit of hell
> I fear more wounds that fester
> And gape, and rot, and smell.

---

44. Interview, Carmine A. Prioli with Ruth Ellen Patton Totten, June 9, 1988.

45. Blumenson, I, p. 520.

> Then here's to blood and blasphemy!
> Then here's to girls and drink!
> In life we know we're living
> In death we only stink.

1918

SOLDIER'S RELIGION

[Somewhat reminiscent of Thomas Hardy's "The Man He Killed,"[46] "Soldier's Religion" is one of Patton's most enigmatic and haunting monologues. The poem expresses the thoughts of an ordinary soldier following a bloody night's duty beyond the front-line trenches, and, like most of the speakers in Patton's verses, this one is a hell-raiser who has never been troubled by the fine points of theology. But an unorthodox religious conversion forces him to wrestle with a series of contradictions between the catechism of the "padres" and the realities of war and survival, contradictions that lead to the poem's unexpected conclusion: that God is somehow present in a confusion of corpses, a mysterious odor, and, most startling of all, in the enemy himself.

In spite of his inability to comprehend the mystery, the speaker in this deceptively subtle poem professes his faith in an uncelebrated God who moves amid the bodies of the fallen in the guise of the common foot soldier. More a throwback to pagan antiquity than to traditional Christianity, the God of "Soldier's Religion" is a battleground deity whose domain is not heaven but No Man's Land, and He appears wherever brave men require solace and encouragement.]

> They made me in my Maker's form?
> Ah! Luckless God that He should be
> Even in so small a thing as shape
> Resembled by a cuss like me.

---

46. Samuel Hynes, ed., *The Complete Poetical Works of Thomas Hardy*, vol. I (Oxford: Clarendon Press, 1982), pp. 344-45.

I have no virtues such as He
At least if as the padres[47] say
He would not even hurt a fly —
I swat a hundred every day.

He does not drink or damn the Boche
He does not smoke or chew
Nor go into "Cat Houses"
To do the things I do.

And yet when I was sitting
In the listening post[48] last night
I sort of felt God near me
And it eased a heap my fright.

The corpses stopped their moving
The wires they whined no more
And a soft warm smell crept o'er me
Like perfume off a whore.[49]

I knew that God was sitting there
And so I wern't afraid
And blowed a stinkin' Hun to hell
With a God-damned hand grenade.

Yet that damned Boche looked just like Him
Leastwise he looked like me
So why God should be partial
I don't just rightly see.

This damned God business may be bunk
I don't just rightly know
Still, when the corpses walk at night
I'd rather believe it's so.

1918

---

47. A chaplain of any Christian denomination. The term "padre" was first commonly used during the American occupation of the Philippines following the Spanish-American War.

48. "Two or three men detailed to go out 'in front' at night, to lie on the ground and listen for any undue activity in the German lines. They also listen for the digging of mines. It is nervous work...." (Empey, p. 298)

49. The reference here is to a prostitute, but Patton could also have been punning on the French term "*hors de combat*," referring to disabled or out-of-action troops.

A World War I American war fund poster commemorating the deaths of the first U.S. soldiers killed in France.
Photo courtesy of James R. Alexander.

TO OUR FIRST DEAD

[Described by Patton as "an effort at blank verse," this poetic elegy to the first American combat deaths of World War I contains one of the General's earliest pronouncements on the "joyous privilege" of dying in battle. It also suggests how apolitical Patton was when it came to fighting. As soldiers "we are not concerned with the causes of war," he wrote in 1919, "for these are provided by statesmen...and are always just."[50] Politicians might justify war on the basis of ideological, territorial or even personal disputes. Dry stuff, relatively speaking.

Patton, on the other hand, was no politician. He would probably have distinguished between the reasons for *declaring* war and the motivations for actually fighting and killing, man to man.[51] For him, life's most meaningful encounter did not commence with words but with blood, the "sacramental crimson" of the great human contest. And despite the General's public pronouncements about winning wars, mere survival was far less important than fighting well. He subscribed to Aristotle's definition of the truly courageous man willing to die a "noble death" in battle. Thus, for Patton a dead hero—whether friend or foe—was to be revered as the greatest inspiration to living warriors. (See also, "A Soldier's Burial," p. 100.)]

(Three soldiers killed by the Germans in a trench
raid in the St. Mihiel sector, November 1917)

They died for France, like countless
    thousands more
Who, in this war, have faltered not to go
At duty's bidding, even unto death.
And yet no deaths which history records
Were fraught with greater consequence than theirs.

---

50. "War As She Is," (manuscript, 1919), Blumenson, I, p. 679.

51. Less than a decade earlier, Patton declared: "I am *not* a *patriot*....I would just as gladly fight for any country against any country, except [the United States]....War is to me simply a matter of business." Letter to Beatrice, January 17, 1909, Patton Papers, Box 6, Library of Congress.

A nation shuddered as their spirits passed
And unborn babies trembled in the womb
In sympathetic anguish at their fate.

Far from their homes and in ungainful strife
They gave their all, in that they gave their life;
While their young blood, shed in this distant land
Shall be more potent than the dragon's teeth[52]
To raise up soldiers to avenge their fall.

Men talked of sacrifice, but there was none.
Death found them unafraid and free to come
Before their God. In righteous battle slain,
A joyous privilege theirs the first to go
In that their going doomed to certain wrath
A thousand foeman for each drop they gave
Of sacramental crimson to the cause.

And so their youthful forms all dank and still
All stained with tramplings in unlovely mud,
We laid to rest beneath the soil of France
So often honored with the hero slain
— Yet never greater so than on this day
When we interred our first dead in her heart.

There let them rest, wrapped in her verdant arms
Their task well done. Now from the smoke-veiled sky
They watch our khaki legions press to certain victory
Because of them who showed us how to die.

1918

REGRET

[Perhaps because his own affluent background was so different from most of theirs, Patton made special efforts to empathize with enlisted men. His frequent and often emotional visits to field hospitals during World War II have been well-publicized, but the General's efforts to identify with his soldiers began during World War I when he absorbed their speech and expressions, imagined their fears, and incorporated them into some of his verses. In 1918 he wrote poems treating what he called "the ideas of many

---

52. The expression "sow dragon's teeth" refers to an action that is intended to put an end to strife, but which brings it about later. It has its origin in the ancient legend of Cadmus, the founder of Thebes, who, after slaying a dragon, sowed its teeth from which sprouted a number of armed men intent upon killing him.

soldiers as expressed in their conversations overheard."[53] In "Regret," for example, we hear the candid thoughts of a tank driver about to move into battle. Although the casualty rate for tank crews was lower than for infantry (approximately 7 1/2% as opposed to 25%),[54] a stalled tank provided an easy target for a direct hit which, in turn, meant certain and instantaneous death.]

> As I sit in my tank and wait for "H"[55]
> Do I regret my past?
> Do I think of the things I shouldn't have done
> And wish I had lived less fast?
>
> I should accordin' to books you read.
> Such books are the work of sluts
> Of driveling, sniveling, snotty swine
> Of bastards without guts.
>
> I do, in fact, regret my past
> The things I failed to do
> The drinks I failed to guzzle
> The pay I never blew.[56]
>
> When a man goes up to face his fate
> What does he really know?
> Except that heaven is probably bunk
> And he's leavin' a damned good show.
>
> Then why should he whine like a craven
> For fears that are mostly fake
> Or howl like a cur on the name of God
> Or babble of Jesus' sake?
>
> It's all very well if I go to Hell
> But I can never drink no more.
> And thinkin' won't ever do no good
> If I can't get in bed with a whore.
>
> So as I slip her into "First"[57]
> And the old barrage comes down
> I wish to God I had one more chance
> Of raising Hell in town.

1918

---

53. "Regret," Patton Papers, Box 60, Library of Congress.

54. Blumenson, I, p. 433.

55. "'H' is the abbreviation for the hour of 'H' or zero hour." (Patton's note.)

56. An earlier version reads: "The girls I failed to screw."

57. "Low gear used to start the tank." (Patton's note.)

THE MOON AND THE DEAD

["The Moon and the Dead" is probably the poem to which Patton referred in a letter to his wife on August 16, 1918: "Here is a poem I wrote a while ago. I went to bed for a while. Did not go to sleep at once so I composed poetry...and rather fancying this I got up and wrote it. It was a moon light night. I think it is rather disconnected, though some of the individual verses sound well."[58]

In the poem, the moon is personified as a woman who sighs for "the lives extinguished," but refuses to grieve for the heroes who have fallen honorably. Although they have lost their lives, their manhood lives on. The image of "gas wreaths" has a number of meanings, the last of which echoes one of Patton's favorite themes: (1) literally they are the poisonous vapors remaining in trenches and shell holes after the gas clouds have blown away; (2) figuratively they are the funeral wreaths of the fallen soldiers; (3) at the same time they come to represent the laurel wreaths of victory.]

> The roar of the battle languished
> The hate from the guns grew still,
> While the moon rose up from a smoke cloud
> And looked at the dead on the hill.
>
> Pale was her face with anguish
> Wet were her eyes with tears,
> As she gazed on the twisted corpses
> Cut off in their earliest years.
>
> Some were bit by the bullet
> Some were kissed by the steel
> Some were crushed by the cannon
> But all were still, how still!
>
> The gas wreaths hung in the hollows
> The blood stink rose in the air
> And the moon looked down in pity
> At the poor dead lying there.

---

58. Blumenson, I, pp. 560-61.

She sighed for the lives extinguished
She wept for the loves that grieve,
But she glowed with pride on seeing
That manhood still doth live.

Yet not with regret she mourned them
Fair slain on the field of strife,
Fools only lament the hero
Who gives for faith his life.

For though the moon is winsome
In wisdom she is old
Nor grudges she the fallen
Nor grieves she for the bold.

Her tears are for the hero
Her hate is for the cur
Her utter loathing for the hound
That shrinks from righteous war.

The moon sailed on contented
Above the heaps of slain
For she saw that honor liveth
And manhood breaths again.

1918

PEACE – NOVEMBER 11, 1918

[The first real opportunity for achieving warrior status came for Patton when he was a Tank Corp commander during the St. Mihiel Offensive in 1918. This campaign began in mid-September and included, in Patton's words, "one fine fight"[59] and an unauthorized tank raid into the Hindenberg line. But on September 26, Patton was wounded. Although his actions up to that time would win him the Distinguished Service Cross – the next best thing to the Medal of Honor – he sat out the rest of the war in military hospitals. When the Armistice was signed on November 11, Major Patton was celebrating his thirty-third birthday and he was miserable. After more than a year's training and preparation, he spent a total of less than five days in actual combat, hardly enough time to prove his mettle.

---

59. Blumenson, I, p. 583.

"Peace was signed....Many flags. Got rid of my bandage."[60] These were the words he penned with uncharacteristic restraint in his diary on the day when most of the world was rejoicing. As he often did in moments of extreme exhilaration or depression, Patton turned to poetry. On this occasion he poured his frustrations into fourteen bitter and dispirited stanzas. Later, when he was editing the poem for publication, Patton was still disheartened by the memory of what might have been, had the war continued. "I would have entrained for the front," he noted at the bottom of the page, "with a new [tank] brigade on the 13th."[61] When Mrs. Patton had a chance to comment on the poem, she wrote simply: "Some of this is grand."[62]]

> I stood in the flag-decked cheering crowd
> Where all but I were gay
> And gazing on their ecstasy
> My heart shrank in dismay.
>
> For theirs was the joy of the "little folk"
> The cruel glee of the weak
> Who, banded together, have slain the strong
> Which none alone dared seek.
>
> The Boche we know was a hideous beast
> Beyond our era's ban
> But Soldiers still must honor the Hun
> As a mighty fighting man.
>
> The vice he had was strong and real
> Of virtue he had none
> Yet he fought the world remorselessly
> And very nearly won.
>
> While the conquerors here – this cheering mob
> With obscene mind and soul
> Who look but on peace as a means to glut –
> Their life's one sensuous goal.
>
> And looking forward I could see
> Life like a festering sewer
> Full of the fecal Pacifists
> Which peace makes us endure.

---

60. Blumenson, I, p. 637.
61. "Peace – November 11, 1918," Patton Collection, U. S. Military Academy Library.
62. *Ibid.*

I saw around the placid hearths of homes
Sleek virtues soft and cheap
Which neither make the soul to soar
Nor cause the heart to leap.

Those bootless, cramping, little lusts
The vices mean and small
Vile scurryings of avarice
Weak lusts by fear held thrall.

None of the bold and blatant sin
The disregard of pain
The glorious deeds of sacrifice
Which follow in war's train.

Instead of these the little lives
Will blossom as before
Pale bloom of creatures all too weak
To bear the light of war.

While we whose spirits wider range
Can grasp the joys of strife
Will moulder in the virtuous vice
Of futile peaceful life.

We can but hope that e're we drown
'Neath treacle floods of grace
The tuneless horns of mighty Mars
Once more shall rouse the Race.

When such time comes, Oh! God of War
Grant that we pass midst strife
Knowing once more the whitehot joy
Of taking human life.[63]

Then pass in peace, blood-glutted Boche
And when we too shall fall
We'll clasp our gory hands as friends
In high Valhalla's Hall.[64]

1918

---

63. In the Library of Congress typescript of this poem, the line "Of taking human life" was stricken out and changed (by a hand that does not resemble Patton's) to: "Of giving life for life." The original must have been a bit too strong for someone, possibly Mrs. Patton, though she had seen and accepted much vintage Patton throughout the years. However, in what appears to be the latest version of the poem in the Patton Collection at West Point, the original line was retained.

64. "Valhalla's Hall," in Norse mythology, is the great hall where Odin, the supreme deity of art, culture, war and death, receives and feasts the souls of heroes who have fallen bravely in battle.

IN MEMORIAM

[On the same day that he wrote "Peace," the General composed a poem in memory of Captain Matthew L. English, a former First Sergeant who served under Patton, commanding a company of tanks. Before he was killed, English had won Patton's respect during the Meuse-Argonne Offensive in September 1918, when the two men braved intense German machine gun fire to help maneuver English's bogged-down tanks forward into battle. For their heroism, both Patton and English were awarded the Distinguished Service Cross. In addition to this poetic elegy for English, Patton wrote a touching letter to the Captain's wife, expressing his "heartfelt sympathy for you and my unbounded admiration for your gallant husband." As a final gesture, he requested that his own wife, Beatrice, also write to Mrs. English.[65]

Patton's high regard for this man was based on the fact that English exhibited the qualities of leadership that became the General's own hallmarks: audacity, visibility and the courage to seek out danger *in front of* his men. In a note to this poem, Patton wrote that English was killed "300 yards ahead of his tanks and the infantry while searching for a passage through a mine field."[66]]

(Capt. Matthew L. English, Co. "C" 344th B., T.C.
Killed in action, Apremont, France, Oct. 4, 1918)

> The war is over and we pass
> To pleasure after pain
> Except those few who ne'er shall see
> Their native land again.

---

65. Blumenson, I, p. 632.
66. "In Memoriam," Patton Collection, U. S. Military Academy Library.

To one of these my memory turns
Noblest of the noble slain
To Captain English of the Tanks
Who never shall return.

Yet should some future war exact
Of me the final debt
My fondest hope would be to tread
The path which he has set.

For faithful unto God and man
And to his country true
He died to live forever
In the hearts of those he knew.

Death found in him no faltering
But faithful to the last
He smiled into the face of Fate
And mocked it as he passed.

No, death to him was not defeat
But victory sublime
The grave promoted him to be
A hero for all time.

1918

BILL

[During the Meuse-Argonne Offensive, Patton commanded one hundred forty tanks, of which forty-three were lost either to enemy action or mechanical failure.[67] Although these armored vehicles worked well against barbed wire, bunkers and machine gun emplacements, they often bogged down in the deep, muddy trenches. Thus immobilized, they became easy targets for artillery, leaving the two-man crew extremely vulnerable to small arms fire if they tried to escape.

---

67. Blumenson, I, p. 619.

In this poem, written as a letter from a wounded tanker to his wife, Patton described some of the perils of the Tank Service. Mrs. Patton noted that the poem was "A favorite of mine."[68]]

> (The incidents here recounted are true and occurred to a crew of one of the tanks of the 304th Brigade, Tank Corps, in September 1918.)[69]
>
> Bill, he kept racin' the motor
> For fear that the damned thing would die
> While I fiddled 'round with the breech block[70]
> And wished for a piece of your pie.
>
> It's funny the way it affects you
> When you're waitin' the signal to go
> There's none of the high moral feelins
> About which the newspapers blow.[71]
>
> For myself I always was hungry
> While Bill thought his spark plugs was foul
> Some guys talks of sprees they's been on
> And one kid, what's croaked, talked of school.
>
> At last I seen "Number One"[72] signal
> I beat on the back of Bill's neck[73]
> He slipped her the juice and she started –
> But Bill he never come back.

---

68. "Bill," Patton Collection, U. S. Military Academy Library.

69. Patton's note. The 304th Brigade was the one Patton organized, trained and led into battle in both the St. Mihiel and Meuse-Argonne Offensives. In addition to the 140 American tanks, Patton also commanded a *groupement* of 28 French army tanks.

70. Part of a machine gun. The crew of the Light Tank consisted of two men, the gunner and the driver-mechanic. The gunner also served as lookout and gave signals to the driver below.

71. Another version of the poem has "padre men" instead of "newspapers."

72. "The platoon commander's tank is Number One." (Patton's note.)

73. "In the Tank Corps the signal to advance is repeated pats on the back." "The noise in a moving tank is so great that the voice cannot be heard; hence, all commands are given by touch signals." (Patton's notes.)

The first news I had of the Boches
Was shot splinters right in the eye
I cussed twice as loud as the Colonel[74]
And clean forgot the damned pie.

A Boche he run out with a tank gun
I gave him a H. E.[75] in the guts
You ought to have seen him pop open!
They sure was well fed, was them sluts.

We wiped out two nests with case shot
An' was just gettin into the third
When we plunked in a hole full of water —
That goddamned Bill sure was a bird.

He hollers to me "Frank, you're married.
"If one of us gets out, it's you."
And he rammed me up through the turret
I guess that's about all I knew...

A stinkin' "whiz-bang" beaned[76] me
Or I might of rescued Bill
But it's too late now, he's sleepin'
By our tank on that goddamned hill.

They gave him the Medal of Honor
For savin' me for you
So if it's a boy we'll name it Bill
It's the least and the most we can do.

1919

---

74. In a note to another version of this poem, Patton wrote: "The Colonel of this brigade was very profane." He was, of course, referring to himself.

75. "H. E. is high explosive shell." (Patton's note.)

76. "Beaned – hit in the head or knocked senseless." (Patton's note.) "Whizbang" was a word of British origin referring to a shell from a German field gun employed for direct fire against troops and tanks. "The whiz of the passing shell and the bang of its explosion hit your ears at practically the same time." (*A Dictionary of Soldier Talk*, s.v. "whizbang.") In his dictionary of the trenches, Empey (p. 314) defined "whizz bang" as "a small German shell which whizzes through the air and explodes with a 'bang.' Their bark is worse than their bite."

A gunner (above) and driver (below) of a Renault tank during World War I.

U.S. Army photo
Courtesy of the Patton Museum

THE YELLOW LEGS[77]

["The Yellow Legs" was Patton's toast presented at a dinner for fourteen cavalry officers, including General Pershing, who served in various capacities (none directly related to the cavalry) in the American Expeditionary Force, and who after the Armistice faced reassignments and uncertain futures. For Patton and his tanks, this uncertainty was especially acute, since tank warfare still existed in a kind of theoretical no-man's land. During the war, tanks were employed as adjuncts to infantry, that is, little more than armored vehicles whose primary function was to clear out machine gun nests and cut through barbed wire. They were not to outpace the slow-moving foot soldiers who flanked and trailed behind them. This limited function failed to exploit the tank's strongest features: mobility and firepower. The war ended before the tankers could perfect either their skills or their machines and, consequently, the science of tank warfare in peacetime America languished for lack of support.

The early lessons of armored and mechanized fighting were not lost on the Germans. By the 1930s their blitzkreig tactics and weapons lay ready to be unleashed on a largely unsuspecting and unprepared world. In part, blitzkreig warfare hinged upon modification of the tank's role from one of support to one of rapid and devasting assault. By 1941 the Allied need for a similar response became apparent after spectacular Nazi successes in France, eastern Europe and northern Africa. At the same time, Patton would be reassigned to the Tank Corps to help orchestrate that response. For the time being, however, it was back to the cavalry, the branch Patton thought most likely to be called up in the war that he wrongly anticipated would soon be declared against Mexico. "The Yellow Legs," written just three days after the Armistice, looks forward to that war, the prospect of which seems to have raised his spirits.]

---

77. "Cavalrymen. So called because of the distinguishing yellow stripe on the breeches of the old blue uniform." (Patton's note.)

(With Apologies to Kipling's "Lost Legion.")[78]

Here's a health to the cavalry soldier
That hard riding, bowlegged wight
Whose soul yearns to battle on horseback
But if need be like a "Dough Boy"[79] he'll fight.
We were crammed with French theories at Riley[80]
We practiced on motors in France
For if horses we lacked for the mounting
In autos we've sure had our chance,
          Dear Boys,
We've all of us taken our chance.

We've painted the Islands vermillion
We've hunted old Pancho to bay
We've skirmished with Mexican bandits
And starved on a Lieutenant's pay.[81]
We've laughed at the world as we found it
Its women and cities and men
We've danced with the Parisian Cocottes
And tea'd with the L. P.[82] Post Hen,
          Dear Boys,
The catty and pious Post Hen.

---

78. Kipling's poem, "The Lost Legion," provided Patton with the meter, rhyme scheme and much of the language for "The Yellow Legs." The extent of his borrowings can be seen by comparing Patton's second stanza with the following lines from "The Lost Legion":

> We've painted The Islands vermillion
> We've pearled on half-shares in the Bay,
> We've shouted on seven-ounce nuggets,
> We've starved on a Seedeeboy's pay;
> We've laughed at the world as we found it,—
> Its women and cities and men—
> From Sayyid Burgash in a tantrum
> To the smoke-reddened eyes of Loben,
>   (Dear boys!),
> We've a little account with Loben.

Rudyard Kipling's Verse: Definitive Edition (New York: Doubleday, Doran, 1940), pp. 194-96.

79. "Infantry soldier. So called because the pipe-clay used to clean the white facings on the old uniform looks like dough when wet." (Patton's note.) This is one interpretation of the origin of "doughboy." The word may also be derived from the flour or corn dumplings made in the field for nineteenth-century infantrymen. Another theory is that the term is related to the *adobe* (pronounced "*dobe*") buildings nineteenth-century soldiers in the American southwest built and inhabited.

80. "The cavalry school at Fort Riley [Kansas], originally based on the French school at Saumur." (Patton's note.)

81. References to the Punitive Expedition (1916-17) against Pancho Villa.

82. "Lady of the Post, sometimes called Leg Puller." (Patton's note.)

The line and the Staff[83] are our portion
And battles at large are our share
For there's never a skirmish to windward
But some of us troopers are there.
Yet, somewhere and somehow and always
We're first where the trouble begins
And we stick to the last due to training
For it's cavalry spirit that wins,
                    Dear Boys,
The son of the horse turd that wins.

Then a health (let us drink it all standing)
To our horsey and masterless herd
To the chiefs of the horse-wrangling troopers
To the cavalry soldier abroad.
Yes, a health to ourselves as we scatter
For now that the Peace dove doth reign
We're through with the Staff and the Tank Corps
We're back to the sage brush again – Regards!
To the cactus and pup-tent again – Hurrah!
To the dust and the desert again – Here's how!
To the trail and the packmule again – Salu!
To the sand of the border again.[84]

1918

---

83. A reference to the headquarters staff of General Pershing to which Patton was assigned before he joined the Tank Corps.

84. Sage brush, cactus, pup-tent and so on are references to duty in Mexico, where hostilities against the U. S. were continuing.

Patton and crew, including Mrs. Patton, on board the *Arcturus*, about to set sail from California to Hawaii in 1935.

Photo courtesy of the Patton Museum

III

1919-1940

INTERLUDE: BETWEEN WARS

Perhaps alone, of all the multitude
My kindred spirit feels their tragic roll
For I, like they, am doomed to stand and gaze
And curb the promptings of my warrior soul.

"The Soul of the Guns"
Captain George S. Patton, Jr.

THE APPROACH MARCH

[Shortly after World War I, but before his return to the Cavalry, Patton was back in the United States where he was appointed to a board of officers investigating ways of improving the tank as a fighting machine. In comparison to the responsibilities he had and the action he saw during the previous year, it was fairly tedious duty.[1] Modifying gearshift mechanisms and conducting test-runs for transporting tanks, for example, did interest Patton, but they hardly compared with training guns and machines upon the German army. As he carried out his stateside duties, Patton's poetic imagination conjured up the more lively memories of St. Mihiel, the Meuse-Argonne, and other war-scarred places that were now associated with his glorious past.]

>Forever the column of panting trucks
>Forever the lines of trees
>Forever the ranks of shuffling men
>Forever the dust-choked breeze.
>
>While far to the front in the flickering light
>Where the sleepless batteries are
>The star flares rise and the cannon roll
>The ceaseless bass of war.

---

1. Blumenson, I, pp. 713-14.

> Above in the maw of the stygian dark
> Sounds the venomous hum of the foe
> While splitting the night come the bursts of light
> Where he drops his bombs in a row.
>
> Now with the first faint signs of dawn
> Like beasts who fear the light
> The columns seek the shell-torn woods
> To hide in their shade till night.
>
> Forever the lines of shattered trees
> Forever the ribbon road
> Forever the mounds and crosses white
> Where men have gone to their God.

1919

A SOLDIER'S BURIAL

[Although he was one of America's most outspoken patriots, Patton defined heroism in a way that raised it above national affiliations. The light of timeless gallantry could outshine allegiance to country and cause; for Patton the interment of a truly brave man was non-partisan and non-sectarian. In a letter to his wife written two weeks before the end of World War I, Patton described the following incident:

> You say the Bosch will quit. Listen to this. One of my tanks was attacking a machine gun when the gun in the tank jammed so the men decided to run down the machine gun. The two Bosch fired to the last and the tank went over them. Next day they were found still holding their gun, though dead.
> There could be nothing finer in war. My men buried them and put up crosses. "Salute the brave," even Bosch.[2]

Thus, the corpse in "A Soldier's Burial" has no national identity or military rank. Patton did write poems eulogizing specific individuals, but here he created his personal model of the Unknown Soldier whose *in memoriam* is not fashioned by the tribute of human institutions. Not man, but Nature properly celebrates his deeds which, with their accompanying "Battle Hymn," had a solemnity of their own. Christian images of ritual and

---

2. Blumenson, I, p. 629.

color run through and help unify this poem, but they are displaced in the final stanza by the mystical "Red Battle's Sun," the celestial artist whose "magic colors" now become the hero's flag.

Published in 1943 in *The Chicago Sun* and the Boston *Record*, "A Soldier's Burial" is one of Patton's best-known works. Mrs. Patton was especially fond of the poem, describing it as "One of my favorites."[3]]

> Not midst the chanting of the Requiem Hymn
> Nor with the solemn ritual of Prayer
> 'Neath misty shadows from the oriel glass
> And dreamy perfume of the incensed air
> Was he interred.
>
> But in the subtle stillness after fight
> In the half light between night and day
> We dragged his body, all besmeared with mud
> And dropped it, clod-like, into the clay.
>
> Yet who shall say that he was not content
> Or missed the priest or drone of chanting choir
> He who had heard all day the Battle Hymn
> Sung on all sides by a thousand throats of fire?
>
> What painted glass can lovelier shadows cast
> Than those the Western skies shall ever shed?
> While mingled with its light, Red Battle's Sun
> Completes in magic colors o'er our dead,
> The flag for which he died.

1943   1919

DEAD PALS

[In October 1919, while stationed near Washington, D.C., Patton wrote a poetic "remonstrance to the transplanting of our dead," by one, he notes drily, "who was nearly planted."[4] Entitled "Dead Pals," the poem speaks for common soldiers and objects to their disinterment in France for reburial in the United States.

---

3. "A Soldier's Burial," Patton Collection, U. S. Military Academy Library.
4. "Dead Pals," Patton Papers, Box 60, Library of Congress.

The lone voice we hear is that of a soldier addressing his comrade who lies buried beside him. Their sacrifice and the values for which they fought become, for Patton, united with the place where they were killed and the manner in which they died. All of this effects a change of allegiances – even nationalistic and familial ties are relinquished as the souls of the dead soldiers become spiritually enfranchised into the brotherhood of the fallen. The voice from the grave says, therefore, that they won't miss the memorial flags and flowers because their "free souls" will be forever defending their positions in France "Where we died to win the war."

The poem, which Mrs. Patton called "One of the best,"[5] also expresses the General's utter disdain for ministers and the hollow sympathy of those who neither understand nor have taken part in the great contest of war. Patton himself had no desire to be buried at home. Like the young man in "Dead Pals," he wished to be interred where he was killed: "That's where any soldier would want to be [buried]," he said; "it will remind people there forever of who it was [who] fought to set them free."[6]

> Dickey,[7] we've trained and fought and died
> Yes, drilled and drunk and bled
> And shared our chuck and our bunks in life.
> Why part us now we're dead?
>
> Would I rot so nice away from you
> Who has been my pal for a year?
> Will Gabriel's trumpet waken me
> If you ain't there to hear?
>
> Will a parcel of bones in a wooden box
> Remind my Ma of me?
> Or isn't it better for her to think
> Of the kid I used to be?
>
> It's true some preacher will get much class
> A-tellin what guys we've been.
> So the fact that we're not sleepin' with pals
> Won't cut no ice for him.

---

5. "Dead Pals," Patton Collection, U. S. Military Academy Library.

6. Ayer, *Before the Colors Fade*, p. 239.

7. A common name for World War I soldiers.

They'll yell, "Hurrah!" and every spring
They'll decorate our tomb
But we'll be absent at the spot
We sought, and found, our doom.

The flags and flowers won't bother us,
Our free souls will be far
Holdin' the line in sunny France
Where we died to win the war.

Fact is, we need no pleasant flowers and flags.
For each peasant will tell his son:
"Them graves on the hill are the graves of Yanks
"Who died to lick the Hun."

And instead of comin' every Spring
To squeeze a languid tear,
A friendly peoples' loving care
Will guard us all the year.

1919

THE SOUL OF THE GUNS

["The Soul of the Guns" is a lament that sets the tone for Patton's most despondent poetic period. Here he identifies with the silent, rusting guns whose "fearful strength" lies dormant in peacetime. In part, the poem echoes the sentiments of the aging warrior of Tennyson's *Ulysses*:

> How dull it is to pause, to make an end,
> To rust unburnished, not to shine in use!
> As though to breathe were life!...[8]

Like Patton and his peacetime army, the guns are "the butt of wanton mirth," derided by crowds who at one time cowered in fear.

Patton's evocation of the "soul" of the guns was more than a simple exercise in anthropomorphism, the projection of human qualities onto inanimate objects to achieve a poetic effect. He saw a kind of spirituality, a timeless divinity in the power they unleashed. For Patton this power was elemental, akin to what he called "the God sent ecstasy of unbridled wrath."[9]

---

8. Alfred, Lord Tennyson, *The Poetical Works of Tennyson*, ed. G. Robert Stange (Boston: Houghton Mifflin, 1974), p. 88, ll. 22-24.

9. Lecture, "The Cavalryman" (1921), Blumenson, I, p. 757.

It was destructive but it was also invigorating, the very source of life for the warrior caste.

The poem is not as much an elegy for the warrior and his "patient friends of steel" as it is a jeremiad, a prophesy of the storm to come when the "laughing" will be the roar of the guns over plains encrimsoned with the blood of the disrespectful crowds. Patton noted that the idea for "The Soul of the Guns" came when he saw some French students "writing foolish remarks on some of their guns returned from the Front."[10]]

> How sad they seem, those rows of rusty guns
> Like patient wounded, helpless under fire;
> And yet more pitiful the guns appear
> In that their fearful strength is still entire.
>
> Poor mighty children of the human brain
> Lacking in naught save in its will to slay;
> Yet doomed to stand, the butt of wanton mirth
> From crowds who lately dared not meet their sway.
>
> Perhaps, alone, of all the multitude
> My kindred spirit feels their tragic roll
> For I, like they, am doomed to stand and gaze
> And curb the promptings of my warrior soul.
>
> But not for long, Oh! patient friends of steel
> Shall we in shameful impotence remain;
> The clouds are gathering which presage the storm
> That sends us, laughing, to the blood-soaked plain.

1919

OUIJA

["Ouija" is one of the fullest expressions of Patton's mysticism. He compares himself as poet to the Ouija planchette used to convey and record messages from the spiritual world. He is merely the "instrument" of a higher force; his poetry is the inadequate rendering of ultimate truth. But the poem also addresses the limitations of other art forms: painting and music, too, are but feeble representations, "poor daubs and discords" of the mysterious

---

10. "The Soul of the Guns," Patton Collection, U. S. Military Academy Library.

"beauties" known by the "Spirit Legions." Put simply, where art fails to capture the highest forms of human expression, then heroic action and duty rightly performed might succeed.]

> It is not I who writes these lays,
> For through my earthly hands
> An unseen spirit puts in words
> His thoughts from viewless lands.
>
> I am the instrument, no more,
> He is the brain and soul
> My hand is guided by his will
> And works to reach his goal.
>
> How sad it is that such gross means
> May scarcely ever show
> The splendid subtle mysteries
> The spirit legions know!
>
> The loveliest blended colors,
> Music's sublimest art
> Are but poor daubs and discords
> To what the ghosts impart.
>
> We can but dimly sense at times
> Like flowering fields afar,
> The beauties of the worlds beyond,
> From whence all beauties are.
>
> Perhaps the ages far ahead,
> Shall make less dense our clay
> So that the light of Spirit truth
> Shall gild at last our day.
>
> 'Till that time comes we can but hope
> At times to faintly see
> The light of knowledge absolute
> Shine dimly, as through me.

1919

PROGRESS

[On October 18, 1919, Patton wrote a letter to his sister that keynoted the despondency that he would feel during the next few years:

> The United States in general and the army in particular [are] in a hell of mess and there seems to be no end to it. We are like people in a boat floating down the beautiful river of fictitious prosperity and thinking that the moaning of the none too distant waterfall – which is going to engulf us – is but the song of the wind in the trees.[11]

Patton was, of course, completely out of sync with the Jazz Age, the period of dissipation and surface gaiety that followed World War I. The lack of apparent discipline that everywhere surrounded him in popular music and dance, painting, poetry and politics, even pervaded the army: "I have been very busy lately trying to teach military art to my officers," he lamented, concluding sourly, "The only one that is profiting is myself."[12]

A short time later, Patton composed "Progress" and "Majority Law." The titles are bitterly ironic, for the poems decry what Patton believed was the retrograde civilization that characterized American life in the 1920s and that, for a time at least, transformed the virile warrior into a prophet of doom.]

> Much have we worshipped our idol of brass
> Taking for diamonds its rhinestone and glass
> Taking for power its monstrous size
> For wisdom the gleam of its porphyry eyes.
>
> Then the pestilence came and afflicted us sore
> And the might of our idol o'er awed us no more.
> We scoffed at his wisdom and spat in his face
> Then sought a new God for the good of the race.
>
> So Despot and Demigogue, Commune and Crown
> Are builded by folly, by folly torn down.
> We love and we squabble, we breed and we die
> And seeking new virtues our old ones decry.
>
> Till at last we shall finish by progress and crime
> In the same formless chaos which started our time.
> And the earth with its millions shall bubble and fade
> To a speck in the vastness from which it was made.
>
> 1920

---

11. Letter to "Nita," Blumenson, I, p. 725.
12. *Ibid*, p. 716.

MAJORITY LAW

They bow to the might and power of law,
To an idol of dung in a garment of straw,
Whose priests are the cravens who dare not behold,
The rule of the strong and the right of the bold.

When the many and foolish the futile and weak,
First banded together their own ends to seek,
They failed in the face of the fearless and few,
Who knew what they wanted and wrought what they knew.

Till at last was conceived in the brain of the crowd,
The theory of TABOO, to hamper the proud,
They dressed it with legends not heard of before,
And bowed to this fiction and called it the LAW.

Till now in the world justice cringes from sight,
While manhood and honor are hid from the light,
And virtue and vigor are withered and sped,
But the LAW – the great fiction – now rules in their stead.

1921

DEFEAT

[Evident everywhere in Patton's writing is the idea that defeat is not physical death but the moral decay of the warrior spirit. Death, in fact, could well be the glorious culmination of a life devoted to manly virtues and martial courage. On the other hand, anything that works to limit or prevent the expression of these qualities – such as compromise or politically motivated decisions to end "righteous" war – works also to encourage their opposite qualities, especially indolence and greed.

Mrs. Patton liked this poem. She declared simply that it was "Good."[13]]

Behold the youth like some fair shining knight
Armed in high ideals, girded for the field
His eyes a-kindle with the patriotic fire
While virtue gilds the blazon on his shield.

---

13. "Defeat," Patton Collection, U. S. Military Academy Library.

His soul aflame with honor yearns for strife
Base means and petty ends he will not see.
"Reform and Honor" is his battle shout.
Would God, fair youth, yours was the victory.

But now alas behold him in the lists
Of mildewed phrase and ancient hackneyed lies
Like some miasma curdling his blood
About him swarm the germs of compromise.

Awhile he battles but soon or late
He notes the glory leaves his blazoned shield
His tainted spirit wearies of the fray
His ideals languish and his virtues yield.

A year perchance of weakening combats pass
Hark to his piping cry of "Compromise"
Behold his armour, now all tarnished brass
While the cold light of greed shines in his eyes.

1921

FLORIDA

[Throughout his life, Patton was an avid saltwater sportsman, and he described fishing as "a great pleasure."[14] In June 1921, while vacationing on the Gulf coast, he wrote three poems: "Florida," "Wigglers" (p.109) and "The Cays (A Fragment)." (p.111) "Florida" may have been written for and sent to Beatrice, an energetic sportswoman in her own right, as an invitation to join him.]

Where the land sloughs off in sand and marsh
And trees grow in the sea.
Where the tarpon leap and the catfish weep,
Come south, come play with me.

---

14. Blumenson, I, p. 468.

By Captiva Bar[15] where the sand crabs are
And the groupers[16] steal the bait,
The jewfish[17] school and lean sharks rule,
Come south, or you'll be late.

To the Boca Pass[18] where the floating grass[19]
And the crabs drift ceaselessly.
Where the tyros[20] shout as the line runs out,
Come south, come play with me.

Where the mangrove shoots its crazy roots
To filch lands from the sea.[21]
Where the pelicans dive and the fish hawks thrive,
Come south, and happy be.

1921

WIGGLERS

[In comparing himself and Beatrice to wigglers – the aquatic larva or pupa of various insects, including the mosquito – Patton wrote what is easily his most fanciful love poem. "Wigglers" appears to have been inspired by Langdon Smith's "Evolution," a poem that begins:

---

15. Off Captiva Island on the Florida Gulf coast.

16. A powerful bottom-dwelling fish. The grouper's unusually large mouth makes it a difficult fish to catch since most hooks tend to be too small. Thus, the inexperienced fisherman is more likely to have his bait "stolen."

17. One of the larger species of grouper, the jewfish can grow to eight feet and weigh 700 pounds. Although there is some evidence that jewfish live in schools, it is popularly believed that they are solitary animals.

18. One of a series of channels west of Ft. Myers.

19. A reference to the sargassum weed that drifts in the Gulf Stream and sustains many forms of microscopic marine life which, in turn, provide forage for larger creatures including crabs, shrimp, triggerfish and sea horses.

20. Novices, amateur fisherman.

21. Patton here refers to the tangle of mangrove roots that extend into the water and trap sediments.

When you were a tadpole and I was a fish
    In the Paleozoic time,
And side by side on the ebbing tide
    We sprawled through the ooze and slime,
Or skittered with many a caudal flip
    Through the depths of the Carbrian fen,
My heart was rife with the joy of life,
    For I loved you even then.[22]]

You can't remember, dearest
For your memory fades too fast,
The beginning of our loving
In the warm and foggy past.

When vapor from the tepid sea
Hung ever in the air,
And rivulets of pinkish mud
Went trickling past us there.

No, you can't remember even
Of the later lukewarm time
When you and I were wigglers,
Wiggling in the pale gray slime.

When our mouths were all our reason
And our bellies all our soul,
When we bred and died and rotted,
By the billion on the shoal.

Yet for ever and forever,
As the cooling waters flow
Past the green of long dead coal fields
Past the continents of snow.

Yes, forever and as truly
As the waters changeless are,
Have I fought for, sought and found thee
As tonight beneath the star.

Ever fearing, ever hoping
Ever winning thee at last,
But to lose thee to regain thee,
In the present from the past.

1921

---

22. Hazel Felleman, *The Best Loved Poems of the American People* (New York and London: Doubleday, 1936), p. 212.

THE CAYS (A Fragment)

["Cays" here (from the Spanish *cayo*, for shoal or rock) refer to the thousands of islets of sand or coral scattered throughout the West Indies. From the fifteenth to the eighteenth centuries, they were the scenes of many bloody encounters, first between the Spanish conquistadors and native inhabitants and, later, between Spanish and English seafarers. (See also "Out of Hell," pp. 126.)]

> Since the pale vagueness of the ancient past,
> When the swart savage sped his hollow tree,
> Through lurid epochs when all-conquering Spain,
> Moved stark and bloody on your sparkling sea.
>
> And later when the ribboned buccaneer
> Held carnival of loot and robbery
> Lighting the sultry blackness of your night
> With flares of burning galleons far at sea.
>
> Till in the latest time of your red past
> The vicious pirate leaguing with the shark
> Made on your pearl-lipped shores his bloody hold
> And in your harbors hid his evil bark.
>
> How often have your trackless, treacherous swamps
> Harked to the cries of ravished nuns in vain,
> How often have your lip-warm waves e'er now
> Sucked to the shark, their bodies free from pain.

1921

THE FORGOTTEN MAN

[Patton's notion of the Western hero is nowhere more evident than in this poem. A combination of Anglo-Saxon and noble savage, he is neither pioneer nor industrialist, but a hunter very much in the sentimental mold of Hawkeye, James Fenimore Cooper's Leatherstocking protagonist. Despite his physical prowess and his mastery of firearms, this typical American hero is a loner, temperamentally and spiritually isolated, and mocked by the encroaching civilization that drives him further and further Westward.

"The Forgotten Man" and "The Vanished Race" (p. 113) were a pair of poems Patton wrote in 1921, portraying the ill-effects of civilization upon the warrior spirit. In both poems, the souls of great conquerors are stifled by "the milling throng," and they yearn for a return to wilderness expanses. In the following year, Patton would again take up this theme and write "The Dying Race" and Rediscovered" (pp. 113 and 114), poems that echo both the language and the dour sentiments of the earlier "uncompleted" studies.

When he wrote these poems, Patton was still going through a period of readjustment. World War I had ended too abruptly for him, before he really had the opportunity to become thoroughly immersed in it. After the war, the National Defense Act of 1920 reorganized the military and abolished the Tank Corps, assigning its personnel to the Infantry. Patton, of course, requested reassignment to the Cavalry where he could play polo ("the nearest approach to mounted combat which can be secured in peace"[23]), participate in horse shows, and hunt. In many ways it was an anachronistic life, but it was not a soft one; and it was the only way this peacetime warrior could exercise certain "Age old" instincts.]

>Not in the jostlings of an alien crowd
>Which blatantly streams through glaring man-made day
>Shall you discover aught of that great race
>Which found and took this land they've ceased to sway.
>
>Their souls are stifled by the milling throng
>Their nostrils cannot brook the foetid air
>Low cunning is abhorrent to their minds
>While clacking gossip drives them to despair.
>
>But where the billowing prairies endless roll
>With ever beckoning urge to top their crest
>They still find scope for their untrammeled soul
>The vast expanses give their spirit rest.
>
>Amidst the trail which tracks the cottonwoods
>Along the turgid river's winding course
>There shall you find the man of hawk-like face
>The man of simple ways and earthbound force.

---

23. George S. Patton, Jr., "Polo in the Army" (paper, 1922), Blumenson, I, p. 765.

And further midst the mountains of the West
Where the lean trail is wet with snow-borne spray
Where soars the eagle o'er the dizzy peak
The pale-eyed conquerors of the world hold sway.

1921

THE VANISHED RACE

Midst the prospect of limitless ridges
In the shadows of measureless peaks
Where the beckoning trail leads onwards
And the echoing silence speaks.

My soul sloughs off the bondage
Of its softly pampered life
My muscles feel the tingle
Of a million years of strife.

Again I have the memories
Of my bodies long since dead
Feel the wholesome righteous loathing
For the peaceful life I've led.

To the mountains and the desert
Age old instinct brings me back
And I find again the wisdom
Which the foetid cities lack.

1921

THE DYING RACE

[A later, slightly different version of "The Forgotten Man" (p. 111).]

Not in the jostlings of an alien crowd,
The turgid streams through blatant midnight day,
Shall you discover aught of that great race
Which found and made this land they cease to sway

The souls of such are stifled by the throng.
Their spirits cannot brook the gilded hall.
Low cunning is abhorrent to their mind.
They die where lack of space would hold them thrall

But where the billowing prairies lowering roll
With ever beckoning urge to top the crest,
They still find space for their untrammeled souls,
Its brown expanses give their spirits rest.

Amongst the trails that track the cottonwoods
Along the muddied river's winding course,
Still shall you find the man of hawk like face,
The man of simple ways and earth born force.

Still further amongst the mountains to the west
Where lean track climbs through the rocky way,
Where rests the eagle on the mountain crests
The pale eyed conquerors of a world hold sway.

1922

REDISCOVERED

When I leave the cold light of the city
Its noise and its hothouse bred men,
Am I quitting the pride of creation,
The perfected end of God's Plan?

Are its women with paint-daubed faces
The creatures God meant them to be?
Are the putty-faced stoopshouldered manlings
His image who died on the Tree?

In leaving such for the deserts,
The mountains and limitless space,
Am I fleeing the vanguard of progress
Or seeking the home of the race?

When the sunrise gilds the snow mountains
While the gulches lie shrouded in gloom,
Where the world stretches downwards forever
From the peaks where the greasewood trees bloom,

I feel, though it may be unrightly,
That 'twas here man's real progress was made,
That 'twas here that the great wisdom found him
And he learned to stand forth unafraid.

'Midst the prospect of boundless ridges
In the shadows of measureless peaks,
Where the beckoning trail leads onwards
And the awful stillness speaks.

My soul sloughs off the bondage
Of its sickly, pampered life,
My muscles feel the tingle
Of a million years of strife.

I have again faint memories
Of my bodies long since dead,
Feel a wholesome righteous loathing
For the city life I've led.

To the mountains and the desert
Age long instincts bring me back,
And I find again the wisdom
Which the painted cities lack.

In the cold light of the summits
The scales have left my eyes
And I know that life is simple
And the manly only wise.

1922

THE CITY OF DREADFUL LIGHT

[Like the frontier heroes Patton idealized in "The Forgotten Man" (p.111) and other poems, the General recoiled at urban life as it had evolved in the first decades of the twentieth century. Preferring the open spaces of land and sea, he often expressed his disgust with what he called the "foetid cities" where, he told Beatrice, "I don't fit but get fits...."[24]

During a visit to Manhattan in 1922, he wrote "The City of Dreadful Light," described by Patton as "the impression of a country boy on viewing the crowd in the largest foreign city in America."[25] Its title suggests that it may have been inspired by "The City of Dreadful Night," a long, intensely pessimistic poem by the English Victorian poet, James Thomson (1834-1882).[26]]

---

24. Letter, March 29, 1909, Blumenson, I, p. 170.

25. "The City of Dreadful Light," Patton Collection, U.S. Military Academy Library.

26. First serialized in the *National Reformer* (London), "The City of Dreadful Night" describes an imaginary place of misery, horror and suicide. Unlike Patton's poem, which is simply an expression of personal distaste for the "mongrel hoard," Thomson's is an extended

On a street of midnight brightness in the city of the damned,
Throngs the choicest of the mongrel hoard we breed;
Chubby women garbed with cunning to arouse the
   beast in man,
Pasty men with questing lecherous eyes of greed.

Carmen-lipped with breasts a-wobble, coarse of ankle,
   huge of thigh,
Cling they vine-like to the things in manwise clothes;
But the manner of their clinging is remindful of a leech,
More like the poison ivy than the rose.

Such a city such a people has dead Carthage known of yore,
Such the creatures to which dying Rome gave birth;
And amongst the failing nations do we find such faces still,
We must change them or give up our place on earth.

Too much ease has bred these vermin, lacking faith and
   force and love,
Bent only now to satiate their lust;
We must cast them from our bosom, we must cleanse the
   wound with fire,
Failing selfhelp 'tis foolish God to TRUST.

                                                    1922

THE WAR HORSES

[Throughout his life, Patton owned horses and, at times, his stables fielded entire polo teams. When it became apparent after World War I that the Tank Corps was not where the nation's military priorities lay, Patton returned to the cavalry; but he always had an opinion about the ways mechanization–on the ground and in the air–was transforming the science of war.[27] In fact, he often noted with pride his initiation of motorized warfare during the Rubio Ranch shootout in 1916. But if Patton's actions in Mexico and, later, in the shell-pocked wildernesses of France predicted the

---

treatment of the spiritual deterioration of an individual psyche. Bertram Dobell, ed., *The Poetical Works of James Thomson*, vol. I (London: Reeves & Turner, 1985), pp. 122-72.

27. The debate between horses and mechanization in the army would continue well into the 1930s with Patton often torn between his fascination with the possibilities of mechanized warfare and his spiritual bond to the horse cavalry, which he saw as a veritable "aristocracy of valor." See Blumenson, I, chaps. 41, 42 and 43.

future fame he would achieve as the premier Allied commander of tanks, his heart was always drawn to the past, to the glories and traditions of military horsemanship, to the headlong, exhilarating cavalry charge, which he saw as the highest expression of courage and moral victory.

Most of the horses used during World War I were not the fleet animals of the cavalry, but they served reliably on the muddy wastelands where motorized vehicles often failed. Moreover, they suffered and, in Patton's eyes, were heartlessly abandoned when the troops came home. "In war, especially, one cannot help admiring the stoicism of horses," wrote another tank commander, British Captain Richard Haigh, in 1918:

> One sees examples of it on all sides. Tread, for instance, on a dog's foot, and he runs away, squealing. A horse is struck by a large lump of shrapnel just under its withers, and the poor brute trembles, but makes no sound. Almost the only time that horses scream – and the sound is horrible – is when they are dying. Then they shriek from sheer pain and fear. Strange as it may seem, one is often more affected by seeing horses struck than when men are killed. Somehow they seem so particularly helpless.[28]]

Where are they now, the horses who fought for us in France,
The horses of the limber[29] and the gun?
They shared our toil and triumph and they shared our joy and pain
But we left them, yes, we left them every one.

I can see them still, all shivering with their rumps set to the rain
On the muddy, cheerless horse lines of the front.
They didn't make a murmur and they took the worst that came
And when they died, they didn't even grunt.

I can see the failing battery on the shell-torn endless roads
Plodding weary through the starless autumn night.
Hear the limber jerk and rattle when the shell holes racked the wheels
But the guns moved on, the guns that won the fight.

When we needed extra rations and the trucks and tractors stuck
The horses bucked the reeling wagons through.
Of their sweat and grief and lifeblood, they gave it without stint
To get a bellyfull for me and you.

But when the war was ended and we heroes hurried home
To learn first hand how laurel wreaths were made,

---

28. Richard Haigh, *Life in a Tank* (Boston: Houghton Mifflin, 1918), pp. 68-69.

29. A two-wheeled vehicle for carrying a gun or caisson.

We left the poor damned horses in an alien, sunless land
So the dealers in the States would lose no trade.

We spent a heap on moving corpses from their graves in France
But for transport for live horses none would vote.
Perhaps they missed the genus of the heroes of the trace[30]
And treated the poor creatures as the goat.

I may be sentimental, or I may be a damned fool
But the horse was treated rotten to my mind.
Forty thousand died to serve us, countless thousands lived to aid
And we left them, left the horses all behind.

1922

THROUGH A GLASS, DARKLY

[The first and twenty-second stanzas of "Through a Glass, Darkly" are quoted by George C. Scott in the movie *Patton*, when he refers to himself in a conversation with General Omar Bradley as "The Poet." The title comes from the First Epistle of Paul to the Corinthians (13:11): "For now we see through a glass, darkly; but then face to face: now I know in part; but then shall I know even as also I am known." The most detailed expression of Patton's lifelong belief in the reincarnation of the warrior spirit, "Through a Glass, Darkly" chronicles human conflict from prehistoric times to the present century and reasserts Patton's grim conviction that this strife will continue into the future. (See also "The End of War," p. 62.)

The poem's details are drawn not from books but from what Patton called his "faint memories" (see "Rediscovered," p. 114) or mental "scars" recalling the most indelible experiences of his previous lives: searing wounds, demented hunger and thirst, blood drops in the snow. He remembered, for example, being a sling-shot soldier with Hannibal, being carried on a shield by four berserkers, and "just a trace" of serving with Lieutenant General Jubal Early in the Battle of the Wilderness during the American Civil War.[31]

---

30. "Trace" refers either to the ground plan of a military installation or, more likely, to the harness straps used to attach a horse to a vehicle or machine.

31. Letter, Ruth Ellen Patton Totten to Carmine A. Prioli, June 25, 1988.

The two final stanzas of this poem illustrate a theme that Patton also explored in "Ouija" (p. 104): he acts merely as the instrument of the spirit world. Because of his "blindness" he cannot understand the divine plan that he is destined to help execute, at times as "hero," other times as "knave." His role as this instrument, however, is not to understand but simply to perform his duty which includes: "Dying to be born a fighter / But to die again once more."]

Through the travail of the ages
Midst the pomp and toil of war
Have I fought and strove and perished
Countless times upon this star.

In the forms of many peoples
In all panoplies of time
Have I seen the luring vision
Of the victory Maid[32] sublime.

I have battled for fresh mammoth
I have warred for pastures new
I have listened to the whispers
When the race track instinct grew.

I have known the call to battle
In each changeless changing shape
From the high-souled voice of conscience
To the beastly lust for rape.

I have sinned and I have suffered
Played the hero and the knave
Fought for belly, shame or country
And for each have found a grave.

I cannot name my battles
For the visions are not clear
Yet I see the twisted faces
And feel the rending spear.

Perhaps I stabbed our Saviour
In His sacred helpless side.
Yet I've called His name in blessing
When in after times I died.

In the dimness of the shadows
Where we hairy heathens warred
I can taste in thought the life blood –
We used teeth before the sword.

---

32. The "victory Maid" refers to Nike, the Greek goddess of victory and her Roman counterpart, Victoria, who was worshipped by the Roman legions.

While in later clearer vision
I can sense the coppery sweat
Feel the pikes grow wet and slippery
Where our phalanx Cyrus met.[33]

Hear the rattle of the harness
Where the Persian darts bounced clear
See the chariots wheel in panic
From the Hoplites'[34] leveled spear.

See the mole[35] grow monthly longer
Reaching for the walls of Tyre
Hear the crash of tons of granite
Smell the quenchless eastern fire.

Still more clearly as a Roman
Can I see the Legion close
As our third rank[36] moved in forward
And the short sword found our foes.

Once again I feel the anguish
Of that blistering treeless plain
When the Parthian showered death bolts[37]
And our discipline was vain.

I remember all the suffering
Of those arrows in my neck
Yet I stabbed a grinning savage
As I died upon my back.

---

33. "Where our phalanx Cyrus met" is a reference to Cyrus the Great (529-553 B.C.), King of Persia, and his conquering of the Greek city-state of Lydia in 546 B.C. A phalanx was an ancient military formation of infantry in close and deep ranks with shields joined together and spears overlapping. Thus, the reference to the bloody pikes that "grow wet and slippery."

34. "Hoplites" were citizens of Greek city-states who could not maintain horses but who had sufficient property to equip themselves with full personal armor. Their chief defence was the heavy bronze shield and they were armed with short swords and nine-foot spears.

35. The "mole" is the causeway built by Alexander the Great during his siege of the Phoenician island-city of Tyre in the year 322 B.C. The capture of Tyre was Alexander's greatest military conquest. After the city fell, 10,000 of its inhabitants were killed and 30,000 sold into slavery. Alexander's causeway remained, turning the island into a peninsula.

36. The "third rank" here refers to the last line of defence in the Roman manipular system of warfare.

37. "Death bolts" refer to the arrows the ancient Parthians shot at their retreating enemies. Thus, the reference to arrows in his neck and to the popular expression, the "Parthian" or "parting shot." Although Patton's early incarnation is described as retreating, he died, we are told, on his back and managed to kill a "grinning savage."

Once again I smell the heat sparks
When my Flemish plate gave way
And the lance ripped through my entrails
As on Crecy's field[38] I lay.

In the windless blinding stillness
Of the glittering tropic sea
I can see the bubbles rising
Where we set the captives free.[39]

Midst the spume of half a tempest
I have heard the bulwarks go
When the crashing, point-blank round shot
Sent destruction to our foe.

I have fought with gun and cutlass
On the red and slippery deck
With all Hell aflame within me
And a rope around my neck.

And still later as a general
Have I galloped with Murat[40]
While we laughed at death and numbers
Trusting in the Emperor's star.

Till at last our star had faded
And we shouted to our doom
Where the sunken road of Ohain[41]
Closed us in its quivering gloom.

So but now with Tanks aclatter
Have I waddled on the foe
Belching death at twenty paces
By the starshell's[42] ghastly glow.

So as through a glass and darkly
The age long strife I see
Where I fought in many guises,
Many names – but always me.

---

38. On August 26, 1346, during the first decade of the Hundred Years' War, Edward III of England defeated the French led by Philip VI at Crecy-en-Ponthieu.

39. Patton here recalls an episode from a previous life as a pirate or privateer witnessing the drowning of captives.

40. Joachim Murat was a leader of cavalry and one of Napoleon's most famous marshals. As a cavalryman in spirit, Patton would have felt a special affinity for this man whose fortunes rose and fell with Bonaparte's. Thus, the reference to "the Emperor's star."

41. Ohain is a town southeast of Waterloo where Napoleon was defeated on June 18, 1815.

42. Starshells were World War I projectiles that detonated in the air, releasing a parachute flare.

And I see not in my blindness
What the objects were I wrought
But as God rules o'er our bickerings
It was through His will I fought.

So for ever in the future
Shall I battle as of yore,
Dying to be born a fighter
But to die again once more.

1922

DECORATION DAY

[From October 3, 1920, until December 18, 1922, Patton commanded a squadron of Cavalry at Ft. Myer, Virginia. Situated just outside of Washington, D.C., the post supplied the U. S. government with sleek horses and impeccably uniformed riders for exhibitions, drills, parades and honor guards. (When he was stationed at Ft. Myer ten years earlier, Patton was selected as the Army representative to ride in the cortege honoring *U. S. S. Maine* sailors whose bodies were retrieved from the sunken vessel and brought to Arlington National Cemetery for burial.[43])

Thus, duty at Ft. Myer gave Patton many opportunities to exercise his passion for horses and military tradition. But the General was no store-window soldier, and without a glorious war to go with them, the colorful uniforms and ceremonies were meaningless sideshows. Stately funeral processions were necessary and desirable accompaniments to war, but they were pallid substitutes for courageous actions on the battlefield. The sideshows became especially galling for Patton who felt that too much attention was afforded to dead heroes and aged veterans, while young warriors like himself served merely as ornaments or, worse, were ignobly shelved like his precious tanks.

"Decoration Day" is one of three "spontaneous" poems that Patton wrote on Memorial Day in 1922 and sent to his wife. The other two are "The

---

43. Carmine A. Prioli, "The Second Sinking of the *Maine*," *American Heritage* 41:7 (November 1990).

Lament of the New Heroes" and "Anti Climax" (p. 124). For Patton, poetry was a vehicle for expressing his most cherished ideals and private thoughts, but he also used it to vent hatred and frustration. Thus, it is in these three poems that he unleashed some of the most churlish exhortations the General ever uttered, in poetry or prose. In the letter accompanying the poems, Patton scoffed: "Having spent the hours from nine to three watching veterans vet, I was so fed up that my poetic soul burst forth with the enclosed."[44]]

> Over the cropped and emerald lawn
> The tiny standards fly
> Marking the graves of fighting men
> Who died as we shall die.
>
> Yet this poor trivial cheap-paid debt
> Is all the mead they gain
> For days of battle agony
> For nights of freezing rain.
>
> 'Tis strange how quick the memory fades
> To bloom again too late
> How quick the living are forgot
> The dead to elevate.
>
> If half the effort, half the cost
> Which yearly decks this sod
> Had been bestowed while life was here
> How great the memory, Lord!
>
> It may not be, our heedless land
> Has ever so repaid
> The men who died to make it
> The men who died to aid.
>
> Since this is so, we can but hope
> That on some future May
> A sweating crowd shall deck our graves
> Whose fathers docked our pay.
>
> 1922

---

44. Letter to "Beatrice," Patton Papers, Box 60, Library of Congress.

THE LAMENT OF THE NEW HEROES

Strange it is how all the glory and the splendor of our youth
Is forgotten with the passing of the need.
While the toothless twisted creature of an era that is gone
Stands before us, the recipient of our mead.

Yes, the lank and scabby creatures who were drafted years ago
Now are lauded and applauded by the throng.
Though the battles which they fought in – if they fought – which none may know
Were as nothing to the fights which we have fought.

Still, we must not wish them evil or begrudge
    them of their fame
For in the future when our vigor too is fled,
We shall strut as now they caper with our toothless jaws adrool
While the fighters of that day shall wish us dead.

'Tis the folly of the ages, all this reverence of the past
This neglecting of the present and the true,
And though we may not like it, we must take it as it comes
But in future claim the same respect of you.

                                                                         1922

ANTI-CLIMAX

[The conclusion of "Anti-Climax," the last of Patton's 1922 anti-Memorial Day poems, restates the ancient warrior conviction that youthful but glorious death in battle is vastly more preferable to mere survival and, later, inglorious senility. To the extent that choice was possible, these were the alternatives offered to soldiers from Achilles[45] to the doughboys of World War I: "When men die for something worthwhile," Coningsby Dawson

---

45. In his speech to Agamemnon's emissaries, Achilles indicated that the Fates have offered him "two sorts" of destinies:

> If I stay here and fight beside the city of the Trojans, my return home is gone, but my glory shall be everlasting; but if I return home to the beloved land of my fathers, the excellence of my glory is gone, but there will be a long life left for me, and my end in death will not come to me quickly.

The Iliad of Homer, Richmond Lattimore, trans., (Chicago: University of Chicago Press, 1952), IX, ll. 411-416. After a good deal of sulking over personal wrongs committed against him, Achilles chooses to avenge the death of his friend, Patroclus, and to die in battle.

wrote from a British military hospital in 1917, "death loses all its terror. It's petering out in bed from sickness or old age that's so horrifying." In what could serve as an apt paraphrase of the final sentiment in "Anti-Climax," Dawson added: "How better can a man shake off his flesh than at the hour when his spirit is most shining?...The vital concern is not *when*, but *how*."[46]]

> 'Tis hard to see in the slobbering lips
> And bleary lashless eye,
> The firm set mouth and eagle gaze
> They had in the days gone by.
>
> Have those scrawny necks like withered kelp
> Ever boomed the deep hurrah?
> Has the shuffling tramp of those dragging feet
> Ever filled a foe with awe?
>
> 'Twere better indeed for the sake of fame
> To have died in the lust of youth,
> Than have lived to wither and drool and blink
> In age's pitiless truth.
>
> Behold yon statue picturing
> A hero slain in strife!
> And then in pity gaze upon
> That comrade still in life.
>
> The one a glorious super-man
> Replete with life and fire;
> The other a poor doddering wraith,
> A witch light in the mire.
>
> And having looked, who can but choose
> To go while life is gay?
> To go while glory gilds the road
> And Victory crowns the day.

1922

---

46. Dawson, *The Glory of the Trenches*, pp. 116, 118.

OUT OF HELL

[Patton's legendary status is based upon his career as an army officer and his genius for conducting ground maneuvers involving tanks and infantry. But the General also had a lifelong love for the sea. He was a strong swimmer, placing fifth out of thirty-seven athletes who competed in the Modern Pentathlon during the 1912 ("Jim Thorpe") Olympics.[47] He was also an avid sportfisherman and an accomplished sailor, who was given his own boat at the age of thirteen. In 1935, with himself as captain and navigator and his wife as a member of the crew, Patton sailed his fifty-two-foot schooner, *Arcturus*, from California to Hawaii. In 1937, he sailed it back again.

So, when Patton wrote "Out of Hell," he began with an historical account of an eighteenth-century sea battle that occurred off Jamaica, but he supplemented it with images from his own seafaring experiences. Moreover, the battle images are expressed with such gory vividness that their sources might have been the flashes that Patton experienced from to time, what he called his "faint memories" of battle encounters in his earlier lives. (See also "Through a Glass, Darkly," p. 118.)

The poem was also inspired by one of Patton's favorite verses, Tennyson's "The Revenge: A Ballad of the Fleet," which he recited for his children with such theatrical effectiveness that, according to his daughter, Ruth Ellen, it was "just like being there."[48] The General's impromptu

---

[47]. The 1912 Games took place in Stockholm, Sweden. The Modern Pentathlon consisted of five events: (1) shooting a pistol at 25 meters, (2) swimming 300 meters, (3) fencing with the dueling sword, (4) riding a 5,000 meter steeplechase, and (5) running a 4,000 meter cross-country footrace. Patton's overall performance was impressive and he might have finished higher had he not inexplicably missed the target in the pistol competition. Martin Blumenson speculates that two of Patton's bullets may have passed through the holes made by previous rounds and therefore could not be counted. In other phases of the competition, Patton was the only fencer to beat the French champion, and he ran so hard in the footrace that he collapsed after crossing the finish line. Blumenson, *Patton: The Man Behind the Legend*, p. 71.

[48]. Letter, Ruth Ellen Patton Totten to Carmine A. Prioli, May 10, 1988.

performances of "Out of Hell" must have been equally spellbinding. Mrs. Patton described the poem as "Great fun!"[49]]

> Historical note: Jamaica, West Indies, A. D. 1700. On June 6, the sloop, *Jennie*, Captain Bolldlock, encountered the Spanish merchantman, *Santa Espala*. A good prize was in prospect when the perfidious Spaniard fired his magazine. All the dons and some of the Free Companions perished in the wreck. May God rest their souls, not those of the Spaniards.[50]

I can feel the heave and settle, I can taste the salty spray
Hear the singing of the back stays in the breeze.
See the little white-lipped islets flitting past us as we speed
Hear the rustling, see the bending of their trees.

I can see the linstocks[51] sparkle as we waved them to make fire
Hear the sizzle of the sparks along our lee,
Where the water rushed a-gutter through the gunports on our quarter
As our falcons[52] dipped their muzzles in the sea.

She was laying dead to leeward as we crashed into her side
And our grapnels caught her forward of the main.
Her nettings went like cobwebs as our boarders leaped the gap.
We were English, we were free men – she was Spain.

Still, the combat was no child's play, they were game, those yellow dogs.
Deep the blue-lipped slits the boarding hatchets made,
While the powder singed our forelocks as we ducked beneath their fire
And their harness turned the keenest rover's blade.

Yet that prize was fairly mastered till that smiling Don stood forth.
Oft we've talked the matter over here in Hell.
How he laid the train of powder that he lit to set her free
How her crashing foremast pinned me as it fell.

There I lay like some snared weasel while she foundered by the stern,
While the creaming water raced along the deck.
Till it showed light green above me and I spluttered out my soul
Bubbling curses to die helpless on my back.

Now in Hell we course and jostle midst the smell of frying flesh

---

49. "Out of Hell," Patton Collection, U.S.Military Academy Library.

50. Patton's note.

51. "The linstocks (matches for the cannon) were waved on going into action to make them burn." (Patton's note.)

52. "Falcons or falconettes were light cannon." (Patton's note.)

Telling tales above the cracklings of the flame.
See the men we stabbed and throttled, kiss the harlots we have drowned
All a-sizzle in community of shame.

1922

THE SOUL IN BATTLE

[Just before he was shot during the Meuse-Argonne Offensive in 1918, Patton had a visionary experience. Pinned to the ground by machine gun fire outside the French village of Cheppy and, as he described it, "trembling with fear," Patton suddenly thought of his military ancestors. "[I] seemed to see them in a cloud over the German lines looking at me," he later wrote. "I became calm at once and saying aloud 'It's time for another Patton to die' called for volunteers and went forward to what I honestly believed to be certain death."[53]

Five of the six men who followed him were quickly killed. Armed with only a walking stick and a pistol, Patton pressed on until he was cut down by a bullet from about forty yards that penetrated his left thigh. Bleeding and immobilized in a shellhole, he used his one remaining soldier, PFC Joseph T. Angelo, to give orders until about twenty-five machine gun nests in the area had been destroyed by Patton's tanks.

The event was a crucial one for Patton because it validated his pedigree as a warrior. It was an initiation rite that linked him with his ancestors, a drawing back of what Patton called the "curtain," giving new vision to the warrior whose eyes have viewed the spirit world lying beyond the "veneer of life."

It is this new vision that Patton attempts to describe in "The Soul in Battle." A kind of brief spiritual testimony, the poem is one he began in 1922 and worked on during the next two years. Despite his efforts, he was dissatisfied with the results. "The idea is here," he grumbled, "but failed to hatch."[54]]

---

53. "My Father," Blumenson, I, p. 613.

54. "The Soul in Battle," Patton Papers, Box 60, Library of Congress.

In the valley of the slaughter where the winged Valkyrie[55] dwell
And the souls of men go naked to their God
I have seen the curtain parted, I have glimpsed the flinty trail
The final road the spirits have all trod.

Yet in the awesome clearness of the future there made plain
The spirit loses something of its dread
And life with all its littleness is very very drab
While the living view the corpses as not dead.

The veneer of life is melted by the hot blast of the shell
And we behold our fellows very plain
Not as cur or fool or hero, but like some poor flustered thing
A trembling beast reluctant to be slain.

1922-1924

FORGOTTEN DWELLINGS

[Reminiscent of earlier poems like "The Fly" and "Mud" (pp. 38 and 53), "Forgotten Dwellings" achieves its shock effect by poetically treating various forms of violent death. Unlike the earlier poems, however, the specific occasion for the composition of "Forgotten Dwellings" has been lost to history. At the time Patton wrote it, he was an officer in charge of personnel and manpower management in Boston, and it is entirely possible that the tedium of a desk job may have elicited the sado-comic element in the General's character. Whatever may have been the occasion for the poem, Patton noted that it was "Incomplete."[56] There is no evidence that he ever returned to it.]

Oh! the corpses of the Arctic, where the stiffening waters surge,
Frozen statues on the ice floes of their doom.
In the semblance of their manhood, 'neath the roseate northern lights,
Wait they patient for the privilege of the tomb.

Oh! the corpses of the South Seas, where the swarming fishes crowd,
To tear and gnaw and suck the still warm husk
Their scattered bones are whitened where the squirming

---

55. In Norse mythology, the maidens of Odin who conduct the souls of those slain in battle to Valhalla, the resting place of warrior spirits.

56. "Forgotten Dwellings," Patton Collection, U.S. Military Academy Library.

sea lice crowd
'Till the grinding billows powder them to dust.

Oh! the corpses in the kelp beds where the storm scourged rollers die,
How they slosh and bob and slither 'midst the weed
With their sloughing eye lids blinking, where the tiny limpits cling
Bob they gruesome as the crabs and sculpin[57] feed.

Oh! the corpses after battle lolling on the oily sea
Where the hunting shark fins periscope the bay,
How their helpless hands wave greeting as the monsters
    drag them down,
While careless dolphins mock them with their play.

                        1924

THE RAPE OF THE CARIBBEAN

[Late in January 1925, Patton was ordered to Schofield Barracks, Hawaii, where he would remain for the next three years. While sailing on the *Chateau Thierry* from New York to Panama, he was impressed by the beauty of the Caribbean, which elicited the following poem. Unusual for its sensuousness, it reveals a side of the General's personality not often seen in his poetry or prose.]

Soft from his island coverts
The sensuous land wind creeps
To stroke the throbbing bosom
Of the dimpling, shuddering deep.

Gently his fragrant fingers
Play with her swelling breast
Till the white nipples gleam in pride
Roused by his soft caress.

Sweet is the breath of his presence
Odor of myriad balms
Mixed epitome of sacred love
And Nature's harlot charms.

---

57. Small, spiny, scaleless fish.

Gently he lays on her bosom
The ripples echo her sighs
While the soft dropping sea mists
Screen their passion from the skies.

1925

THE PACIFIC

[In February 1927, Patton received urgent messages requesting him to come to the family home in California where his father was seriously ill. As he sailed from Hawaii on board the *S. S. Maui*, Patton wrote "The Pacific," a poem heavily influenced by the sentimental nature poets of a century earlier. When Patton arrived in California, he found that his father's condition had improved, but the prospect of Mr. Patton's death seemed to have put his son in an unusually meditative and philosophical mood.]

Oh! waters which have lapped the questing prows
Of far flung argosies in days of yore
Or crept in bustling ripples through lagoons
To filch the lovelorn secrets of the shore.

Or yet again in frenzied majesty
Have loosed your wind-lashed courses o'er the deep
'Gulfing in rain 'neath their changing lives
The hapless mariners to weed-wrapped sleep.

Voice for our benefit your long romance
Recite the tales of continents now sped
Limn for our eyes that long-departed race
Whose deathless monoliths still guard their dead.[58]

Oh! what a story could you not disclose
Of valor, love, of yearning and despair
If for a day your sphinx-like ripples spoke
And deigned an answer to our curious prayer.

1927

---

58. A reference to the centuries-old gigantic stone figures marking the sacred burial grounds of Easter Islanders.

Col. and Mrs. Patton attending a costume ball as King Arthur and Guinevere in 1939.

Photo courtesy of Martin Blumenson
and Ruth Ellen Patton Totten

THE SWORD OF LONO

[While on board the *S. S. Maui*, Patton also wrote "The Sword of Lono," a poem that shows the influence of Mrs. Patton's research in Hawaiian culture and folklore. She assembled a collection of legends which she translated into French and later published as *Blood of the Shark* (1936).[59] In "The Sword of Lono," Patton combined his belief in reincarnation with elements of the legendary Excalibur, King Arthur's magical sword, the medieval Crusades, and the saga of Lono, a Hawaiian warrior deity.[60]

After 1927, Patton's activities were varied and productive. He worked on amphibious assault operations, invented a new machine gun mount, wrote lengthy reports on training, leadership and military history. He also advocated the use of armored cars and half-tracks in cavalry maneuvers, and he developed a renewed interest in tanks. After "The Sword of Lono," however, Patton apparently wrote no poetry until the commencement of World War II, which would prove to be the greatest and final chapter of his life. It would also be an occasion when his poetic muse would visit him once again, if only sporadically.]

> Long have I wandered since, in far castle,
> Fire and the anvil joined to give me birth
> And I appeared a vivid thing of steel
> To 'grave my fame in blood o'er half the earth.
>
> First in a soldier's hand I felt the thrill
> Of ringing combat as we stormed a town
> And drank my fill of blood as through the dawn
> We slaughtered Moors to give our Queen her crown.
>
> Again in memory I seem to feel
> My keen point bite the Unbelievers' mail
> The kiss of frenzied parries as he strove
> Toward my lunge and strove to no avail.
>
> There on a ship I wandered many a day
> Stopping at times to drink some savage gore
> Until at last I came, all white with brine,
> Strapped to a corpse, to rest on Maui's shore.

---

59. See also Mrs. Patton's *Legendes Hawaiiennes* (Paris: Les Belles Lettres, 1950).

60. See Martha Beckwith, Hawaiian Mythology (New Haven, Conn.: Yale University Press, 1940), Chap. III, "The God Lono," pp. 31-41.

A rescued sailor polished there my blade
And long I served him, Lono, white and fair
While as a god he ruled a savage race
Nor failed I, in his hand, his fame to share.

On many a field I flashing led our van
And many a dark-skinned chief to carrion sped
In every isle I quenched my baleful thirst
Great was my fame, great as the list of dead.

But glory passes and in Lono's death
The clumsy savage little knew my worth
My blade was shattered and in evil hour
I came to stand the sign of God on earth.

Yet soon their childish memory failed to link
My twisted hilt with that white blade of yore
And cast to earth in miserable disgrace
My rusty grip was trampled by the shore.

But though a shapeless wreck I now appear
Midst spear and adze for crowds to look upon
I still am Lono's sword and in his hand
I was the means to all the fame he won.

1927

IV

1941-1945

WORLD WAR II

For in war just as in loving, you must always keep on shoving
Or you'll never, never get your just reward.
For if you are dilatory in the search for lust or glory
You are up shitcreek, and that's the truth, Oh Lord!

"Absolute War"
Lieutenant General George S. Patton, Jr.

TIME
THE WEEKLY NEWSMAGAZINE

THIRD ARMY'S PATTON
The enemy has reason to fear him.
(*World Battlefronts*)

On April 9, 1945, during the heat of spectacular Allied victories in Europe, *Time* magazine ran a feature article on Gen. Patton, saying that he "was definitely in nomination for Public Hero No. 1 of the war." Effusive in its praise for Patton, the magazine further noted: "Even the Germans help to glorify him. Some enemy officers and men consider it more honorable to have had to surrender to 'Bloody' Patton's Third Army."

Copyright 1945 Time Warner Inc.
Reprinted by permission.

THAT MUST BE BENSON
OR
WHERE IN THE JEBYL[1] *IS* BENSON?

[On July 15, 1940, Patton was on leave at his home in South Hamilton, Massachusetts. While reading the morning newspaper, he saw an item about himself and discovered to his surprise that he had been assigned to a tank division.[2] The post was of tremendous importance to Patton who, after many years of being a "potbound" soldier, would again have the chance to lead men and tanks in battle. It was also a sign that the U. S. Army was making up for lost time. With their blitzkrieg attacks, the Germans had already defeated Poland and France, and had succeeded in driving the British from the European continent.

During the next two years, Patton mastered some of the German techniques of armored warfare, and he molded the 2nd Armored Division "from an idea to a powerful fighting force."[3] With master strokes of public relations, he gained widespread publicity for himself and his tankers, and by November 1942, Patton and his army of 24,000 men were poised to attack North Africa in "Operation Torch," at the time the largest amphibian assault in history. "All my life," he wrote, "I have wanted to lead a lot of men in a

---

1. Patton is here punning the words "devil" and "djebel," an Arabic term for hill. Djebel Chemsi and Djebel Ben Kreir, for example, were important map locations during the Battle of El Guettar.

2. Blumenson, I, p. 955.

3. Blumenson, II, p. 25.

desperate battle."[4] Now he had his chance. On November 8, 1942, Patton's forces landed. Three days later, on his fifty-seventh birthday, they took Casablanca.

For the next ten months, Patton occupied himself with the relatively mundane business of establishing a military stronghold in Morocco. His next opportunity for combat did not occur until March 1943, when Allied forces hunted General Erwin Rommel in Tunisia. Patton was ordered to rehabilitate the American II Corps, recently bloodied at the Kasserine Pass, in conjunction with British troops under Sir Harold Alexander.

The Allied operation, later to be known as the battle of El Guettar, was launched on March 16. Whenever he could, Patton left the safety of his command post to maintain visibility with his front-line combat troops. During one of these forays, Patton–who was now a three-star general–descended upon an assault led by his old World War I friend, Colonel Chauncy C. Benson. When he arrived, Patton found Benson's leading units halted at a mine field. Furious, Patton himself directed the tanks across. Benson's force went on that day to make contact with the British Eighth Army, and along the way it captured over a thousand prisoners. At that point, Patton's fighting in Tunisia was over. Next day, he wrote his first poem in many years, a satirical account of some of the confusion he saw during Colonel Benson's operation. He sent a copy of the poem to his wife, saying it was about "Chauncy reporting himself one place when he was at another and getting shelled by us."[5] An error in map reading placed Benson's unit seven miles north of his actual position.]

---

4. Blumenson, II, p. 92.

5. Letter, June 6, 1943, Patton Papers, Box 13, Library of Congress.

I

The forward observer clearly saw
Thirteen tanks in a wadi-draw[6]
"Help!" he hollered in the 608[7]
"Shoot 'em now or it'll be too late.

"At five thousand yards I can't be wrong –
"They look too low and they look too long."
Up jumped the General[8] and he said, said he
"Where in the Jebyl can Benson be?"

II

"Benson, boys," the G-2[9] said,
"Tells me daily where he means to head.
"Today as usual, and he's never late,
"He's smack on grid-line Thirty-Eight."[10]

So Reaper reported without delay,
"Battalion, three rounds, on the way."
Then up bounced Benson, and he said, said he,
"Whose in the Jebyl can those rounds be?"

III

Buzz went the phone and buzz went the wire
And buzz went my ear with a loud "Cease fire!"
"I know blame well," said the voice, "this party
"Can't be Jerry – it's Irwin's Army."[11]

"Now Chauncy," said the General, half-irate,
"Aren't you fighting this out on Thirty Eight?"
"Our fire's at fifty," said Benson, "Ah, me.
"Where in the Jebyl can Three Eight be?"

1943

---

6. A dry ravine.

7. An army telephone.

8. The "General" here is Patton.

9. "G-2" is the designation for the military intelligence officer.

10. "Grid line Thirty-Eight" is a map reference.

11. "Jerry" is a reference to the Germans. "Irwin" probably does not refer to Erwin Rommel, but to Stafford Leroy Irwin, an artillery officer of the 9th Division in Tunisia, later commander of the 5th Infantry Division in Patton's Third Army.

General Patton after the Sicilian campaign in 1943. He is being accompanied on the piano by an Italian prisoner of war.
U.S. Army photo

GOD OF BATTLES

[As early as 1918 in "Soldier's Religion" (p. 77), Patton had created a unique version of God for the ordinary combat soldier; but the most controversial and public version appeared in a prayer published in the November 1943 issue of *Woman's Home Companion*. Entitled "God of Battles," the prayer was heavily influenced by Kipling's "Hymn Before Action."[12] However, unlike Kipling's appeal to "Jehovah of the Thunders," Patton's prayer-poem was a sonorous invocation to a warrior-diety whose avatar was General Patton himself. (See frontispiece.)

The portrait of Patton (which is printed in red) shows him wearing his insignia of rank, necktie and steel helmet. He is dressed for battle in his characteristic spit-and-polish uniform, and the expression he bears is his "war mask," which as Martin Blumenson has asserted, he cultivated "to inspire his soldiers and, incidentally, himself."[13]

Was this identification of Patton with the "God" of battles merely another example of the General's audacious and undisguised egotism? He may not have intended exactly this sort of association, but there is no evidence that he objected to it. In fact, after seeing the poem in print with his portrait, he told Mrs. Patton that it was "pretty good."[14] And just a few months earlier in his diary, Patton mused: "All the men steal looks at me – it is complimentary but a little terrible. I am their God or so they seem to think."[15]

Clearly, Patton was exploiting a kind of hero worship he perceived and cultivated in his men. But "God of Battles" also had a deeply personal significance. His triumphs in North Africa convinced Patton that he was the ablest commander the Allies could put up against the Axis powers. The

---

12. See *Rudyard Kipling's Verse: Definitive Edition* (New York: Doubleday, Doran, 1945), pp. 323-24. Patton's prayer also echoes, at least in its title, King Henry V's apostrophe to the "God of Battles" on the eve of the English army's meeting the French at Agincourt on October 25, 1415. See Shakespeare's *Henry V*, IV, i, ll. 306-22.

13. Martin Blumenson, *The Many Faces of George S. Patton, Jr.* (Colorado Springs, CO: U. S. Air Force Academy, 1972), p. 17.

14. Letter to Beatrice, November 11, 1943 (Patton's fifty-eighth birthday), Patton Papers, Box 13, Library of Congress.

15. "Diary," July 3, 1943, Blumenson, II, p. 270.

doubts and insecurities that had plagued him all his life finally disappeared. Now the face he wore onstage and—more permanently—in "God of Battles" epitomized what the General had earlier called "the secret of victory," the embodiment of a lifetime's determination "to acquire the warrior soul."[16]

After seeing "God of Battles" in *Woman's Home Companion*, a reader wrote to Mrs. Patton: "Every American should be proud of the praying, fighting, poetic General Patton."[17] One month later, the poem was set to music and broadcast for the troops in Europe by the American Expeditionary Radio Station. (See Introduction, p. xiii.)]

> From pride and foolish confidence
> From every weakening creed
> From the dread fear of fearing
> Protect us, Lord, and lead.
>
> Great God, who through the ages
> Hast braced the bloodstained hand,
> As Saturn, Jove or Woden
> Hast led our warrior band.
>
> Again we seek Thy counsel,
> But not in cringing guise.
> We whine not for Thy mercy—
> To slay: God make us wise.
>
> For slaves who shun the issue
> We do not ask Thy aid.
> To Thee we trust our spirits,
> Our bodies unafraid.

---

16. Blumenson, I, p. 798. See also Patton's lecture (p. 723) to his officers (1919) in which he tells them that they are "not only members of the oldest of honorable professions, but are also the modern representatives of the demigods and heroes of antiquity."

17. Blumenson, II, p. 367.

> From doubt and fearsome 'boding
> Still Thou our spirits guard,
> Make strong our souls to conquer,
> Give us the victory, Lord.[18]

1943   n.d.

SEVEN UP!

[Patton's accomplishments in North Africa were merely a prelude to what was to come a few months later when on July 10, 1943, he led 200,000 soldiers of the American Seventh Army in the invasion of Sicily. Before setting out, he lectured some of his men, saying that battle was "the most magnificent competition in which a human being can indulge. It brings out all that is best," he proclaimed, "it removes all that is base."[19] The fall of Palermo, the spectacular race to Messina, and the taking of nearly 100,000 prisoners in some five weeks made Patton and his Seventh Army household names in America.

---

18. Late in 1944, an Army chaplain who was compiling the *Soldier's and Sailor's Prayer Book*, asked Patton to write a prayer. The General's contribution was somewhat more conventional than "God of Battles," but it revealed Patton's unmistakable touch in every line:

A SOLDIER'S PRAYER

God of our Fathers, who by land and sea has ever led us on to victory, please continue Your inspiring guidance in this the greatest of our conflicts.

Strengthen my soul so that the weakening instinct of self-preservation, which besets all of us in battle, shall not blind me to my duty to my own manhood, to the glory of my calling, and to my responsibility to my fellow soldiers.

Grant to our armed forces that disciplined valor and mutual confidence which insures success in war.

Let me not mourn for the men who have died fighting, but rather let me be glad that such heroes have lived.

If it be my lot to die, let me do so with courage and honor in a manner which will bring the greatest harm to the enemy, and please, oh Lord, protect and guide those I shall leave behind.

Give us the victory, Lord. (Blumenson, II, pp. 393-94.)

Patton was also credited with the famous prayer for good weather on the eve of the relief of Bastogne. In fact, the prayer was written by Chaplain James O'Neill. (Blumenson, II, pp. 605-606; also Farago, *Ordeal and Triumph*, p. 690 and Patton, *War As I Knew It*, p. 175, n1.)

19. Blumenson, II, p. 269. Also, pp. 398, 421, 718.

A study in contrasts: Lt. Gen. Mark W. Clark, Commanding General of the U.S. 5th Army, and Lt. Gen. Patton, at the time Commanding General of the U.S. 7th Army, waiting for President Franklin D. Roosevelt at the airport in Castlevetrano, Sicily, December 8, 1943. Unlike the understated and strictly functional uniform of Gen. Clark, Patton's uniform displays the General's characteristic flair: personal touches include the "Sam Browne" belt, oversized stars, and, pinned to his right pocket, military insignias awarded by the Sultan of Morocco. The dagger indicates that Patton was an honorary corporal in the Ghomier Army.

U.S. Army Photo
Courtesy of the Patton Museum

At the same time that Patton was becoming his country's most heroic officer, he jeopardized his future by committing two serious indiscretions. These were the notorious and highly publicized "slapping" incidents that took place in August at the height of the Sicilian campaign. During two of his frequent visits to army field hospitals, Patton struck with his gloves two enlisted men suffering from combat fatigue but who, the General believed, were malingerers. Patton's actions prompted Allied Commander Eisenhower to place his most successful General – and his friend – in mothballs for awhile.

As a result, Patton watched idly for the next five months while the war continued. It was during this desolate and uncertain period that he wrote "Seven Up!" His reference in the poem to the Army's chief being made a "permanent" alludes to Patton's own recent nomination for promotion to the permanent (retirement) rank of Major General. It is also a pun on "permanent wave," a hairdo made solely for the purpose of looking pretty. The "others hurrying past him" refer to Patton's rival, General Mark Clark, and the American Fifth Army, which had been given the task of invading the Italian mainland, a mission Patton desperately wanted for himself.

The title, "Seven Up!" is a take-off on the popular soft drink, while the poem itself is an adaptation of Stephen Foster's popular song, "Nelly Was a Lady." (See Introduction, p. v.) In the last stanza Patton predicts that the Seventh Army, reduced from nearly a quarter million to less than five thousand men, would rise again as the legendary Phoenix rose from the ashes. He was wrong. It would not be the Seventh, but the U. S. Third Army that he would eventually train and unleash in France and Germany.]

> Once there was an Army
> Then one day it died
> So toll the bell and waken Hell
> To give it room inside.
>
> The story of this Army
> Is very very drear
> Its beginning and its ending
> Were especially queer.

> They made its chief a *permanent*[20]
> So he perchance could *wave*
> At others hurrying past him
> Their country for to save.
>
> But now just like a skeleton
> Upon the desert floor
> Orders like vultures come each day
> To pick away some more.
>
> The thing has got so very bad
> That now his friends suspect
> That he no longer can command
> Even his self-respect.
>
> Yet like the fabled Phoenix
> The Seventh shall arise
> Again to soar in triumph
> Through flaming smoke veiled skies!

1943

ABSOLUTE WAR

[The invasion of Hitler's Fortress Europe had taken place in June 1944, but Patton played no role in it. Still sidelined following the slapping incidents in Sicily, Patton was being saved for later action. By the end of July, a beachhead against the Germans had been well established, and Patton was turned loose as Commander of the American Third Army. In two weeks Patton would write that they had killed five thousand and captured thirty thousand German soldiers, and that his forces had advanced "farther and faster than any Army in the history of war."[21]

On the eve of his spectacular success in France, Patton wrote "Absolute War." It expresses his frustration with the slower, more methodical brand of warfare as practiced by, among others, Patton's British rival, General Bernard L. Montgomery. But the poem was also a kind of poetic pep talk, intended to translate into the language of the common

---

20. Because of the controversy surrounding the slapping incidents, Patton's promotion was held up. He was not officially a Major General until August 16, 1944.

21. "Diary," August 14, 1944, Blumenson, II, p. 510.

soldier a sentiment of Georges Jacques Danton (1759-94), a French orator and military leader, whom Patton was especially fond of (mis)quoting: "L'audace, l'audace, toujours l'audace."[22] (Boldness, boldness, always boldness.)]

> Now in war we are confronted with conditions which are strange
> If we accept them we will never win.
> Since by being realistic, as in mundane combats fistic
> We will get a bloody nose and that's a sin.
>
> To avoid such fell disaster, the result of fighting faster
> We resort to fighting carefully and slow.
> We fill up terrestial spaces with secure expensive bases
> To keep our tax rate high and death rate low.
>
> But with sadness and with sorrow we discover to our horror
> That while we build, the enemy gets set.
> So despite our fine intentions to produce extensive pensions
> We haven't licked the dirty bastard yet.
>
> For in war just as in loving, you must always keep on shoving
> Or you'll never never get your just reward.
> For if you are dilatory in the search for lust or glory
> You are up shitcreek and that's the truth, Oh Lord!
>
> So let us do real fighting, boring in, gouging, biting.
> Let's take a chance now that we have the ball.
> Let's forget those fine firm bases in the dreary shell-raked spaces,
> Let's shoot the works and win, yes, win it all!

1944

THE LIFE AND DEATH OF COLONEL GASENOYL: AN EPIC POEM OF THE GREAT WAR OF 1944

[In the Patton Papers at the Library of Congress, this version of "The Life and Death of Colonel Gasenoyl" is mimeographed in typical army fashion on legal-size paper. Thus, many copies are likely to have been run off and distributed. No author is listed, but the poem is collected with the General's other verses. Moreover, the original misspellings and the bawdy,

---

22. Actually, "De l'audace, et encore de l'audace, et toujors de l'audace." ("Boldness, and again boldness, and always boldness.")

Lt. Gen. Patton awarding the Distinguished Service Cross to his old friend, Col. Harry A. "Paddy" Flint. Flint's helmet displays the insignia of his regiment: AAAO, meaning "Anything. Anywhere. Anytime. Bar Nothing." He sent this photo to Patton and wrote on the back: "I had rather have this medal pinned on by you than anyone else I know."

U.S. Army photo
Courtesy of the Patton Museum

satirical, scatological style are vintage Patton. Additionally, Patton had already created an earlier fictional counterpart of Colonel Gasenoyl in a paper he published in 1924. Entitled "Armoured Cars with Cavalry," it opened with a futuristic fantasy starring a "Lieutenant General Alonzo B. Gasoline."[23]

Colonel Gasenoyl may have been modeled after either Colonels "Paddy" Flint or Harry Semmes, both World War I comrades of Patton and both the kind of rugged commanders the General admired. They, in turn, practically idolized Patton. When Semmes heard of the General's appointment as a commander of tanks in 1940, he returned to active duty to serve under his old friend. Semmes went on to distinguish himself while leading a tank unit against the Vichy forces in Morocco. In a letter to Eisenhower, Patton wrote that at Port Lyautey, Colonel Semmes used eight tanks and two or three armored vehicles to attack "18 French tanks with their accompanying infantry, destroying 6 and driving the others back about 8 kilometers with heavy losses to the infantry." "During this fight," Patton continued with apparent pride, "Colonel Semmes' tank was hit three times in the first five minutes, and Colonel Semmes, himself, using his M.37 [anti-tank gun] accounted for four French tanks...."[24]

Paddy Flint's accomplishments were even more daring. In a letter to Beatrice five days after Patton's spectacular capture of Messina, the General described a typical Flint *coup de théâtre*:

> At Troina, Paddy Flint got out in front of his men, stripped to the waist and armed only with field glasses. The Germans were shooting at fairly close range, so Paddy stood on a rock, rolled a cigarette with one hand, and called out to the Germans. "Shoot, you bastards, you can't hit me." This so inspired his men that they gave a yell and took the position. Paddy was not touched.[25]

A year later, Flint was killed in action during the invasion of France. With admiration (and some envy), Patton noted that his friend was shot in the head at "short range" by a pistol bullet, indicating that Flint was engaged

---

23. "Armoured Cars with Cavalry," *The Cavalry Journal* 33: 134 (January 1924), 5-10.
24. Blumenson, II, p. 115.
25. Letter, August 23, 1943, Patton Papers, Box 13, Library of Congress.

in close fighting.[26] Colonel Semmes survived the war and went on to write a biography of Patton.[27]

What makes "The Life and Death of Colonel Gasenoyl" controversial for its time is that the "Great War" referred to in the subtitle is between the Americans and the Russians, herein described as "Reds." Patton's desire to go after the Soviet army in World War II when he finished with the Germans was well-known. It was also one factor that led to his final humiliation, his removal after the European war as Commander of the Third Army.]

(By one who is fed up on mechanization.)

In Nineteen Hundred and forty four
Our land was swept by cruel war
Such parlous times
These halting rhymes
Can only indicate, no more.

As usual our land defense
Had been cut down to save expense
To a squad or two
Which even you
'll admit is not much armaments.

This paltry force was much despised,
But the enemy was soon surprised,
For the Cavalry
Was a sight to see,
This cavalry was mechanized!

Aloysius Gasenoyl,
Defender of his native soil!
Colonel of the Horse
In the mechanized force!
Stout Aloysius Gasenoyl!

He led his troops to the battle scene,
He led them full of gasoline,
"Now hark to me,"
Says Colonel G,
"I want to tell you what I mean."

---

26. Blumenson, II, p. 487.
27. Harry H. Semmes, *Portrait of Patton* (New York: Appleton-Century-Crofts, 1955).

"The Country's honour is at stake!
"Sic Semper Tempus,"[28] thus he spake,
The meaning of which
The son-of-bitch
Had no idea, but it sounded great.

The soldiers loved old Colonel G,
No greater man, they thought, than he,
But a soldier's fate
Was now in wait,
For that mechanical S-O-B.

The Reds now charged with vim and glee
Can Openers they wielded free
And these they sank
In car and Tank
Which much disgusted Colonel G.

Oh! What a horrid scene was there
Where once had been so brave and fair!
Oil and blood
Were mixed like mud
The fumes of gas were everywhere.

But the saddest sight of all to see
Was the pitiful plight of Colonel G,
A wounded Titan
Through with fightin'
His dying words were, "God damn me."

"No more my bonny black-eyed wench'll
"Wait her brave bridegroom potential,
"A bullet stray
"Has carried away
"My drive shaft and my differential!"

Friends, shed a tear for that poor old man!
No braver soldier ever ran.
His friends concurred
He should be interred
With honours full in a kerosene can.

— — —

---

28. Gasenoyl's version of John Wilkes Booth's cry after he shot Abraham Lincoln. "Sic semper tyrannus" ("Ever so to tyrants") is the motto of the Commonwealth of Virginia.

Part II – He Rises From the Grave

They bury him and his moustaches
But Gasenoyl gets up and dashes
For another can.[29]
That deathless man
Rose up like Phoenix from the ashes.

"It is not death that's stalking me
"My bowels are just a trifle free!
"An easy mistake
"For a man to make
"Confusing Death with Diarrhea.

"I grant you that my wounds are sore,"
He shouted through the back-house door.
"But what I've lost,
"At trifling cost,
"Can be replaced at a Hardware Store."

The troops set up a raucous cheer
Their war-cry: "Gasenoyl and Beer!"
Rings through the land
When through that band,
A group of messengers appears.

"In recognition of your toil,
"Fighting for your native soil,
"The Congress voted
"You're promoted.
"HAIL! GENERAL GASENOYL!"

Epilogue

Advancing then, the message holder
Pinned a spiral gear upon his shoulder.
Thus a general's grade[30]
The old man made
While seated on a seven holer.[31]

1944

---

29. That is, a commode.

30. A single star would normally indicate the rank of Brigadier General. In Gasenoyl's case, the spiral gear (a gear in which the teeth are cut at an angle) is more appropriate.

31. An Army latrine.

Lt. Gen. Patton serving the first piece of the victory cake celebrating victory in Sicily to Col. "Paddy" Flint, September 1943. The dagger-pin on Patton's shirt indicates his status as an honorary corporal in the Ghomier army.

U.S. Army photo
Courtesy of the Patton Museum

REFERENCE: B AND B3c-24614
FILE: INV. FORM A62B-M. Q.

[The exact date of the composition of "Reference" is unknown, but the line stating that "Vict'ry is in sight" indicates that the poem was probably a product of early 1945. Like so many of Patton's poems, the meter and rhyme scheme are imitative of Kipling, whose works accompanied the General throughout 1944 and 1945. (See Introduction, p. vii n5.)

Although the real-life identity of "Morton Quirk," the poem's "Hero," remains a mystery, he could have been any one of a plague of bureaucratic busybodies who afflicted Patton throughout his military career. The General was a perfectionist in most things, but he was obsessed with getting done whatever assignment he was given, quickly and efficiently. He therefore had little patience with the red tape created by desk-bound soldiers and civilians.]

>As Head of the Division of Provision for Revision
>Was a man of prompt decision – Morton Quirk.
>Ph.D. in Calisthenics, P. D. Q. in Pathogenics
>He has just the proper background for the work.
>
>From the pastoral aroma of Aloma, Oklahoma
>With a pittance of a salary in hand
>His acceptance had been whetted, even aided and abetted
>By emolument that netted some five grand.
>
>So, with energy ecstatic this fanatic left his attic
>And hastened on to Washington, D.C.
>Where with verve and vim and vigor, he went hunting for the Nigger
>In the woodpile of the W. P. B.[32]
>
>After months of patient process Morton's picular[33] proboscis
>Had unearthed a reprehensible hiatus
>In reply by Blair and Blair to his thirteenth questionnaire
>In connection with their inventory status.
>
>They had written – "Your directive when effective was defective
>"In its ultimate objective – and what's more
>"Neolithic hieroglyphic is, to us, much more specific
>"Than the drivel you keep dumping at our door."

---

32. War Production Board.

33. A Patton neologism, both a pun on "peculiar" and "piculet," a woodpecker. "Blair and Blair" is as yet unidentified.

This sacrilege discovered, Morton fainted – but recovered
Sufficiently to write, "We are convinced
"That sabotage is camouflaged behind perverted persiflage.
"Expect me on the 22nd inst."

But first he sent a checker, then he sent a checker's checker
Still nothing was disclosed as being wrong.
So a checker's checker's checker came to check the checker's checker
And the process was laborious and long.

Then followed a procession of the follow-up profession
Through the records of the firm of Blair and Blair.
From breakfast until supper some new super-follow-upper
Tore his hair because of Morton's questionnaire.

The file is closed, completed, though our Hero, undefeated
Carries on in some Department as before.
And Vict'ry is in sight of – not because of – but in spite of
Doctor Morton's mighty efforts in the war.

1945?

OH, LITTLE TOWN OF HOUFFALIZE

[On December 16, 1944, Hitler ordered infantry and panzer divisions westward from Germany into Belgium's Forest. The surprise counter-attack, which came to be known as the Battle of the Bulge, penetrated fifty miles into Allied territory. It lasted exactly one month and cost thousands of lives before the Germans were pushed back nearly to where they started. By January 16, 1945, the German line lay just eastward of Houffalize, a Belgian town that was devastated during the conflict. In his diary, Patton noted with awe that the town was "completely removed," adding "I have never seen anything like it in this war."[34] Channeling his wonder into a Christmas carol, he composed the following grim parody of "O, Little Town of Bethlehem."]

>Oh little town of Houffalize,
>How still we see thee lie;
>Above thy steep and battered streets
>The aeroplanes sail by.
>
>Yet in thy dark streets shineth
>Not any goddamned light;
>The hopes and fears of all thy years,
>Were blown to hell last night.

1945

---

34. Blumenson, II, p. 632.

Homecoming for the conquering hero. Gen. Patton arrives in Boston on June 7, 1945, following World War II. He is greeted by his wife, Beatrice.

U.S. Army photo
Courtesy of the Patton Museum

THE SONG OF THE BAYONET

[General Patton had a special affection for the idea of hand-to-hand combat, and at one time even taught the proper use of the bayonet. He lectured that the psychological effect of this weapon was much more devastating than the physical harm it might inflict upon an enemy. "Few men are killed by the bayonet," Patton wrote, "[but] many are scared by it."[35]

Although "The Song of the Bayonet" was written in 1920, it was one of the poems Mrs. Patton attempted to have published in 1945. (See Introduction, pp. vii-viii.) No one knew the General as thoroughly as did Mrs. Patton, and her efforts on behalf of this poem were consistent with Patton's own successful attempts to forge a public image based on what might be called his "bayonet psychology," that is, the demoralization of the enemy through fear.

Since no other Allied commander could inflict destruction as rapidly and as certainly as could Patton, even the rumor of his presence was a formidable weapon. One of the most effective Allied deceptions of the war, therefore, involved the creation of a fictitious army in England with Patton as its "commander." Everything from bogus camps to false radio traffic to pre-invasion type bombing patterns were used to convince the Nazi High Command that the forces of operation "Fortitude" were massing in Dover for an invasion of the Pas de Calais.

As a result, the German Fifteenth Army was poised to meet the non-existent "Army Group Patton," when Allied forces actually landed farther south on the Normandy beaches on D-Day, June 6, 1944. "It is the apparent menace of death," Patton noted in 1926, "rather than actual death which wins battles."[36]]

> From the hot furnace, throbbing with passion
> First was I stamped in the form to destroy.
> And the fierce heat of my birth has removed
> Out of my heart every wish but one joy.

---

35. Patton, *War As I Knew It*, p. 386.

36. Blumenson, I, pp. 802-803.

> Carefully tempered was I, and well-sharpened
> Ever and always pursuing my trust.
> How have I yearned as we rushed on the dummies
> For the hot draught at the end of the thrust.
>
> Deep in the faggots and sacks have I burrowed[37]
> Seeking still vainly to slake my long thirst.
> Gouging and prodding the dummies with venom
> Viciously, stubbornly doing my worst.
>
> Then on a morning, wet and o'er clouded
> Was my long hunger sated at last.
> Deep in his entrails the short lunge had sent me,
> Rich was the blood of my final repast.

1920

FEAR

["Do not take counsel of your fears" was one of the most frequent aphorisms heard by Patton's officers and enlisted men. Echoing voices from antiquity to Franklin Delano Roosevelt, Patton spoke with authority and with the experience of one who, for all of the confidence he had in his "destiny," experienced deep fear before every major competition and battle. "My old fear of fear came up again today,"[38] he wrote at the beginning of the battle of El Guettar. But as always for Patton, once the fighting was underway his fear dissipated.

When he decided to write about the subject poetically, Patton chose to personify fear, to concretize it for his readers rather than simply to speak about fear in the abstract. In doing so, he enabled his readers to deal more effectively with their own deep-seated apprehensions. The strategy here is a simple one: to externalize the "enemy," to cloak it in an identity distinct from one's own, an evil to be vanquished on the psychological battlefield with courage and self-discipline.

---

37. "Dummies on the bayonet assault courses are made either of bundles of twigs or else sacks full of sand." (Patton's note.)

38. Letter to "Beatrice," March 30, 1943, Blumenson, II, p. 202.

Although "Fear" was written in 1920, it joined the company of the General's published poems when it appeared in *Cosmopolitan* in March 1945. The magazine paid him $250 for it.[39] Mrs. Patton called this poem "One of my favorites."[40]]

> I am that dreadful, blighting thing
> Like rat-holes to the flood
> Like rust that gnaws the faultless blade
> Like microbes to the blood.
>
> I know no mercy and no truth
> The young I blight, the old I slay
> Regret stalks darkly in my wake
> And Ignominy dogs my way.
>
> Sometimes in virtuous garb I rove
> With facile talk of easier way
> Seducing, where I dare not rape
> Young manhood from its honor's sway.
>
> Again in awesome guise I rush
> Stupendous, through the ranks of war
> Turning to water with my gaze
> Hearts that before no foe could awe.
>
> The maiden who has strayed from right
> To me must pay the mead of shame
> The patriot who betrayed his trust
> To me must own his tarnished name.
>
> I spare no class, or cult, or creed
> My course is endless through the year
> I bow all heads and break all hearts
> All owe me homage – I am FEAR!

1945   1920

---

39. Blumenson, II, pp. 654.

40. "Fear," Patton Collection, U. S. Military Academy Library.

General Patton shortly after World War II, wearing a distinguished lifetime's worth of awards and decorations, many from foreign governments.
U.S. Army photo
Courtesy of the Patton Museum

DUTY

[As he always did, Patton credited his greatest successes to his officers and men. On March 23, 1945, the day before his triumphant urination in the Rhine, he issued the following General Order to the Third Army:

> In the period from January 29 to March 22, 1945, you have wrested 6,484 square miles of territory from the enemy. You have taken 3,072 cities, towns, and villages....
>
> You have captured 140,112 enemy soldiers and have killed and wounded an additional 99,000, thereby eliminating practically all of the German Seventh and First Armies. History records no greater achievement in so limited a time....
>
> The world rings with your praises....[41]

"Duty" is one of Patton's undated poems, but its reference to "this bloody war today" and its upbeat, almost euphoric note indicate that it could only have been inspired by the spectacular successes of the Third Army. For once, Patton felt that he was living up to his destiny, to the high expectations that others – especially his wife – had of him.

But the General's euphoria would not last. His sensational battlefield triumphs helped to speed the end of the war, the one thing that made his life meaningful. On August 10, 1945, he wrote to his wife: "Last time a war stopped I wrote a poem 'Then pass in peace blood glutted Boche, etc.' {see "Peace," p. 84.} Now I feel too low. It is hell to be old and passé and know it."[42]

On December 9, 1945, Patton was injured in a car accident in which he sustained head lacerations and a broken neck. Although paralyzed from the chest down, he remained conscious and lucid for nearly two weeks, when it became increasingly clear that the end would not come, as he had always hoped, from the "last bullet of the last battle." He had outlived his wars only to face death as a total invalid, on his back, his head braced in traction by cables and hooks embedded in his skull. "This is an ironical thing to have to happen to me," he said without apparent bitterness to one of his doctors. Just after 6 a.m. on December 21, he died from congestive heart failure and a

---

41. Blumenson, II, p. 660.

42. Box 16, Patton Papers, Library of Congress.

large pulmonary embolism. According to his final wishes, the General was buried in a military cemetery at Hamm, Luxembourg, among the fallen soldiers of his Third Army. Since 1945 his grave has been moved twice to accommodate the growing number of visitors.

It is fitting that "Duty" may have been General Patton's last poem.]

> Duty that armed Abraham's hand
> And nerved the blade of Antony
> Thy lambent light n'er brighter burned
> Than in this bloody war today.
>
> It steadies in its darkest hour
> The wavering heart of woman-hood
> It makes the boy to sacrifice
> His life, his all for country's good.
>
> Oh! mighty soul, uplifting thought
> That did inspire the great of yore
> Thou hast returned into our midst
> Pray God thou ne'er shall leave us more.

1945?

SELECTED BIBLIOGRAPHY

"Allies Squeeze the German Bulge." *Life* (cover). January 15, 1945, pp. 15-21.

"Armored Force." *Life* (cover). July 7, 1941, pp. 72-89.

Army Times, Editors. *Warrior: The Story of General George S. Patton.* New York: Putnam's, 1967.

Ayer, Fred, Jr. *Before the Colors Fade – Portrait of a Soldier: General George S. Patton, Jr.* Boston: Houghton Mifflin, 1964.

Bernhardi, Friedrich von. *Britain as Germany's Vassal.* (Original title, *Our Future – A Word of Warning to the German Nation,* 1912.) J. Ellis Barker, trans. London, 1914.

Blumenson, Martin. *The Many Faces of George S. Patton, Jr.* Colorado Springs, CO: U.S. Air Force Academy, 1972.

_____. *Patton: The Man Behind the Legend.* New York: William Morrow, 1985.

_____. *The Patton Papers: 1885-1940.* Boston: Houghton Mifflin, 1972.

_____. *The Patton Papers: 1940-1945.* Boston: Houghton Mifflin, 1974.

Bourke-White, Margaret. *"Dear Fatherland, Rest Quietly."* Chap. 3, "A Last Look at George Patton." New York: Simon and Shuster, 1946.

Bradley, Omar N. *A Soldier's Story.* New York: Holt, Rinehart & Winston, 1951.

Chown, Jeffrey. *Hollywood Auteur: Francis Coppola.* New York: Praeger, 1988.

Codman, Charles R. *Drive.* Boston: Little, Brown, 1957.

Coffman, Edward M. *The Old Army: A Portrait of the American Army in Peacetime, 1784-1898.* New York: Oxford University Press, 1986.

Creel, George. "Patton at the Pay-Off." *Collier's.* January 13, 1945, pp. 24-25, 60.

Current, N. *Secretary Stimson: A Study in Statecraft.* New Brunswick, NJ: Rutgers University Press, 1954.

Dawson, Coningsby. *The Glory of the Trenches.* New York: John Lane, 1918.

Dormer, Elinore M. *The Sea Shell Islands: A History of Sanibel and Captiva.* New York: Vantage Press, 1975.

Dow, George F. *Every Day Life in the Massachusetts Bay Colony.* 1935. Rpt. New York: Dover, 1988.

Eisenhower, Dwight D. *At Ease: Stories I Tell to Friends.* Garden City, NY: Doubleday, 1967.

Elting, John R., Dan Cragg and Ernest L. Deal. *A Dictionary of Soldier Talk.* New York: Charles Scribner's, 1984.

Empey, Arthur Guy. *Over the Top.* New York & London: G. P. Putnam's, 1917.

Erbsen, Claude E. "Old Blood and Guts." *Weekly Philatelic Gossip.* November 21, 1953, pp. 366-69.

Essame, H. *Patton: A Study in Command.* New York: Charles Scribner's, 1974.

Evans, Rowland, Jr. and Robert D. Novak. *Nixon in the White House: The Frustration of Power.* New York: Random House, 1971.

Farago, Ladislas. *The Last Days of Patton.* New York: McGraw-Hill, 1981.

_____. *Patton: Ordeal and Triumph.* New York: Ivan Obolensky, 1963.

Felleman, Hazel, ed. *The Best Loved Poems of the American People.* New York and London: Doubleday, 1936.

Field, John. "Patton of the Armored Force." *Life.* November 30, 1942, pp. 113-14, 116-18, 121-22, 124-25.

"Flash Gordon." *The New Yorker.* November 11, 1944, p. 25.

Forty, George. *Patton's Third Army at War.* London: Ian Allen, 1978.

Fritz, Florence. *The Unknown Story of World Famous Sanibel and Captiva (Ybel y Cautivo).* Parsons, WV: McClain, 1974.

"George S. Patton, Jr., Soldier, Diplomat, Poet." *Los Angeles Graphic.* June 23, 1917.

Halsey, Ashley. "Ancestral Gray Cloud Over Patton." *American History Illustrated.* March 1984, pp. 42-48.

Hardy, Thomas. *The Complete Poetical Works of Thomas Hardy*. Ed. Samuel Hynes. Oxford: Clarendon, 1982.

Harkins, Paul D. *When the Third Cracked Europe: The Story of Patton's Incredible Army*. Harrisburg, PA: Stackpole Books, 1969.

Hatch, Alden. *George Patton: General in Spurs*. New York: Julian Messner, 1950.

Hofstadter, Richard. *Social Darwinism in American Thought*. Rev. ed. New York: George Braziller, 1969.

Hogg, Ian V. *The Biography of General George S. Patton*. Greenwich, CT: Bison Books, 1982.

Hollenback, Karl F. "Patton: Many Lives, Many Battles." *Venture Inward*. September/October 1989, pp. 12-14, 49.

The Howitzer: Annual of the United States Corps of Cadets. West Point, NY: U.S. Military Academy, 1909.

Irving, David. *The War Between the Generals: Inside the Allied High Command*. New York: Congdon & Lattes, 1981.

Jaeger, Werner. *Paideia: The Ideals of Greek Culture*. Gilbert Highet, trans. 3 vols. New York: Oxford University Press, 1943-1945.

Johnson, Gerald W. "Prometheus Patton." *Virginia Quarterly Review* 21:2 (1945), pp. 273-80.

Kant, Immanuel. *Perpetual Peace*. Louis White Beck, ed. Indianapolis and New York: Bobbs-Merrill, 1957.

Kipling, Rudyard. *A Choice of Kipling's Verse*. Ed. T. S. Eliot. 1941. London: Faber and Faber, 1976.

_____. *Rudyard Kipling's Verse: Definitive Edition*. New York: Doubleday, Doran, 1945.

Lattimore, Richmond, trans. *The Iliad of Homer*. Chicago: University of Chicago Press, 1951.

Leckie, Robert. *Delivered From Evil: The Saga of World War II*. New York: Harper & Row, 1987.

Linenthal, Edward Tabor. *Changing Images of the Warrior Hero in America: A History of Popular Symbolism*. New York and Toronto: The Edwin Mellen Press, 1976.

Link, Arthur S., ed. *The Papers of Woodrow Wilson*. Vol. 33. Princeton, NJ: Princeton University Press, 1980.

Look (cover). June 1943.

Macaulay, Thomas Babington. *Lays of Ancient Rome*. Philadelphia: E. H. Butler, 1853.

Mellor, William Bankcroft. *Patton, Fighting Man*. New York: Putnam's, 1946.

Newsweek (covers). July 26, 1943; August 28, 1944; January 8, 1945.

Nye, Roger H. *The Patton Mind: The Professional Development of an Extraordinary Leader*. New York: Avery, 1990.

Overbeck, S. K. "Total Warrior." *Newsweek*. October 7, 1974, p. 98.

Patton, Beatrice Ayer. *Blood of the Shark: A Novel of Old Hawaii*. Honolulu: Paradise of the Pacific Press, 1936.

_____. *Legendes Hawaiiennes*. Paris: Les Belles Lettres, 1950.

_____. "A Soldier's Reading." *Armor: The Magazine of Mobile Warfare* 61:6 (1952): 10-11.

Patton, George S., Jr. "Armored Cars with Cavalry." *The Cavalry Journal* 33:134 (1924): 5-10.

_____. "Fear." *Cosmopolitan*. May 1945, p. 37.

_____. George S. Patton Papers. Library of Congress, Washington, DC.

_____. "God of Battles." *Woman's Home Companion*. November 1943, p. 19.

_____. *Helpful Hints for Hopeful Heroes*. Washington: HQ, U.S. Army Ground Forces, 1946.

_____. Patton Collection. U.S. Military Academy Library, West Point, NY.

_____. *War As I Knew It*. Boston: Houghton Mifflin, 1947.

Prioli, Carmine A. "King Arthur in Khaki: The Medievalism of General George S. Patton, Jr. "*Studies in Popular Culture* 10:1 (1987): 42-50.

_____. "The Poetry of General George S. Patton, Jr." *Journal of American Culture* 8:4 (1985): 71-82

_____. "The Second Sinking of the *Maine*." *American Heritage* 41:8 (December 1990).

Province, Charles M. *The Unknown Patton*. New York: Hippocrene, 1983.

Semmes, Harry H. *Portrait of Patton*. New York: Appleton-Century-Crofts, 1955.

Service, Robert W. *The Complete Poems of Robert Service*. Dodd, Mead, 1944.

Shale, Richard. *Academy Awards: An Ungar Reference Index*. New York: Ungar, 1978.

Shane, Ted. "Patton." *The Saturday Evening Post*. February 6, 1943, pp. 19, 81-82.

Sidey, Hugh. "The Presidency: 'Anybody see *Patton*?'" *Life*. June 19, 1970, p. 2B.

Song and Service Book for Ship and Field. New York: Barnes, 1942.

"The Star Halfback." *Time* (cover). April 9, 1945, pp. 33-36.

Stevenson, Burton Egbert. *The Home Book of Verse, American and English*. 2 vols. 9th ed. New York: Holt, 1953.

Tennyson, Alfred, Lord. *The Poetical Works of Tennyson*. Ed. G. Robert Stange. Boston: Houghton Mifflin, 1974.

Thomson, James. *The Poetical Works of James Thomson*. Bertram Dobell, ed. London: Reeves & Turner, 1895.

A Treasury of Stephen Foster. New York: Random House, 1946.

Wellard, James. *General George S. Patton, Jr.: Man Under Mars*. New York: Dodd, Mead, 1946.

Whiting, Charles. *Patton's Last Battle*. New York: Stein & Day, 1987.

Williams, Vernon. *Lieutenant Patton and the American Army in the Mexican Punitive Expedition, 1915-1916*. Austin, TX: Presidial Press, 1983.

Williamson, Porter B. *Patton's Principles*. Tucson, AZ: Management and Systems Consultants, Inc., 1979.

INDEX

Page numbers in italics refer to illustrations.

A

Academy Awards ("Oscars"), xix, xix n33
Achilles, 124, 124 n42
aerial warfare, 9
Alexander, Sir Harold, 138
Angelo, Joseph T., 128
Arcturus (Patton's schooner), 14, *95*, 126
Aristotle, xv, xvii, 80

B

Benny, Jack, xiv
Benson, Chauncy D., *see* "That Must Be Benson," 137-139
Bernhardi, Friedrich von, *Britain as Germany's Vassal*, xii-xiii, 62; *The War of the Future*, xii n16
Bible, ix n5
Blumenson, Martin, x, xxi, 73, 141
Book of Common Prayer, ix n5
Boyd, Carl, 59
Bradley, Omar N., 118
Brooks, Phillips, "O, Little Town of Bethlehem," vi, 155
Bulge, Battle of, 155
Burns, Robert, "To a Louse," 4 n6, 38

C

Caesar, *Commentaries*, ix n5
Cárdenas, Julio, 19
Carlyle, Thomas, xii
Chiriaco Summit, CA (Patton Museum), xviii
Clark, Mark, W., *144*, 145
Codman, Charles, x
Collier's, ix, xv
Cooper, James Fenimore, 111
Coppola, Francis Ford, xviii, xix n32
Cosmopolitan, *see* "Fear," 158-159
Cronkite, Walter, xviii

D

Dante, 7
Danton, Georges Jacques, 147
Dawson, Coningsby, *The Glory of the Trenches*, 54, 124
D-Day, 157
Distinguished Service Cross, awarded to Matthew L. English and Patton, 87

E

Early, Jubal, 118
Eisenhower, Dwight D., 149
  reprimanding of Patton, viii,
  sidelining of Patton, 145
El Guettar, battle of, *see* "That Must Be Benson," 137-139
Eliot, T. S., xviii
Empey, Arthur Guy, *Over the Top*, 71
English, Matthew L., *see* "In Memoriam," 87-88

F

Fifth Army, 145
Flint, Harry A. ("Paddy"), *see* "The Life and Death of Colonel Gasenoyl," 147-152, *148*, *153*
Florida, *see* "Florida," 108-109 "The Cays (A Fragment)," 111
Ford, Henry, 20-21
Ft. Meyer, VA, xi, 122

Ft. Riley, KS, 93 n80
Ft. Sheridan, IL, 15
"Fortitude" (bogus WW II operation with Patton as "commander"), 157
Foster, Stephen, "Nelly Was a Lady," vii-viii;
see "Seven Up!" 143-146

G

Gasoline, Alonzo B. (fictional character created by Patton), 149
Gettysburg, battlefield, 22
Gilbert and Sullivan, vi
"Gothas" (German twin-engine bombers),
see "Mud," 53-55
"Dusk," 56
"The Air Raid," 57
Goumiers, *144, 153*

H

Haig, Sir Douglas, 53
Haigh, Richard, *Life in a Tank*, 117
Hamm, Luxembourg (Patton's burial site), 162
Hardy, Thomas, "The Man He Killed," 77
Hawaii, folklore of,
see "The Sword of Lono," 133-134
Henry, Patrick, xx
Hitler, Adolf, ix, xvii n27, 146, 155
Holbrook, Hal, xviii
Home Book of Verse, vi
Homer, iv, *Iliad*, v, 124 n42
Hope, Bob, xiv
Houffalize, Belgium,
see "Oh, Little Town of Houffalize," 155
The Howitzer (West Point yearbook), 6, 71 n38

I

Irwin, Stafford Leroy, 139 n111

J

Johnson, Gerald W., xx
Jolson, Al, xiv

K

Kant, Immanuel, 32; *Eternal Peace (or Perpetual Peace)*,
see "The Curse of Kant," 34-35
Keats, John, *Endymion*, 7 n14
King Arthur, 133, *217*;
see "Oh, Ye Foolish Half-God Mortals," 13-14
King, Martin Luther, Jr., xx
Kipling, Rudyard, vi, viii, xviii n5, 154;
"The Song of Deigo Valdez," v;
"The *Mary Gloster*," 61 n16;
"The Lost Legion," 93 n78;
"Hymn Before Action," 141

L

Langres, France, 61, 69
Liszt, Franz, Liebesträume, xv
Longfellow, Henry Wadsworth, vi

M

Macaulay, Thomas Babington, vi,;
Lays of Ancient Rome, 25 n45
Maine (battleship), 122
Manhattan, NY,
see "The City of Dreadful Light," 115-116
Matassa, Corporal, xvii
Meuse-Argonne Offensive (WWI), 19, *50*, 87, 88, 89 n69, 99, 128
Mexico, 19, 28, 30, 38, 40, 92, 94 n84, 116

Moltke, Helmuth von, xii
Montgomery, Sir Bernard L., 146
Morpheus (god of dreams), 39
motorized warfare, 19, 68, 116-117
"Musical Review" (dedicated to Patton), xv

N

Newsweek, xix
Nixon, Richard, xix
North Africa, invasion,
   see "That Must Be Benson," 137-139

O

Olympics (1912), 126 n47
"Operation Torch" (N. Africa invasion), 137

P

Patton (film), xviii-xix,
   see "Through a Glass, Darkly," 118-122
"Patton" (M-46 tank), xviii
Patton, Beatrice Ayer (wife),
   ix, xv, 3, 7, 15, 28, 38, 61, 76, 83, 86 n63, 87, *96*, 100, 108, 115, 123, 133, 138, 142, 149, *156*, 157, 161;
   evaluations of husband's poetry, 20, 58, 85, 89, 101, 102, 107, 127, 159;
   as Guinevere, 14, *132*
marriage, 13, 37
  poems written for:
  "Beatrice," 7-8
  "To Beatrice," 36-38
  "Rubber Shoes," 60
  "To Your Picture," 72-73
  "Wigglers," 109-110
Patton, George Smith (father), v, xii-xiii, 30, 131;
   attitude toward son's poetry, viii, 6, 30

Patton, George Smith, Jr.,
  frontispiece, *xxiv*, *18*, *27*, *43*, *67*, *96*, *132*, *136*, *140*, *144*, *148*, *153*, *156*, *160*
as actor, xiv
as aide to Pershing, *43*
ancestors, 11 n22, 44, 128
anti-materialism,
  see "Valor," 20-22
  "L'Envoi," 25-26
  "Youth," 35-36
  "Progress," 105-106
anti-pacifism,
  see "Valor," 20-22
  "Eternal Peace," 32-34
  "The Curse of Kant," 34-35
  "The End of the War," 62-64
anti-populism,
  see "The Rulers," 22-25
  "Majority Law," 107
  "The Forgotten Man," 111-113
  "Rediscovered," 114-115
  "The City of Dreadful Light," 115-116
as archeologist, 65
and art, limitations of,
  see "Ouija," 104-105
and automobiles, 19, 60
"bad" poems, xxi
and battle as "magnificent competition," xiii
"bayonet psychology," xvi-xvii;
  see "The song of the Bayonet," 157-158
"Blood and Guts" (nickname),
  see "Old Blood and Guts"
blitzkreig tactics, 137-138
and bureaucrats,
  see "Reference," 154-155
and cadet life,
  see "A Toast," 3-4
  "The Five Stages of Cadet Life," 4-5
  "The Life of a Cadet," 6-7
as cavalryman, 112, 116-117, 122;

(Patton, George, Smith Jr.)
   see "The Yellow Legs,"
     92-94
  and ceremonies,
    see "Decoration Day,"
     122-123
  and cities,
    see "The Vanished Race,"
     113
    "Rediscovered," 114-115
    "The City of Dreadful
     Light," 115-116
  and clergymen, 102, 143 n18
  commemorative postage
    stamps of, xix
  and common soldier,
    empathy with
    see "Regret," 81-82
    "Bill," 88-90
    "Dead Pals," 101-103
  death of, 161-162
  and destiny, 33, 61, 74, 158,
    161
  depression, viii, 6, 8, 30, 161,
    see "Peace--November
     11, 1918," 84-86
    "The Soul of the Guns,"
     103-104
    "Progress," 105-106
  disillusionment,
    see "Progress," 105-106
     "Majority Law," 107
     "Defeat," 107-108
  and "divine beauty," 7
  and duty, 105,
    see "Duty," 161-162
  dyslexia, xxii
  egotism, 141, x
  and emotion, x, 15 n32
  and evolution,
    see "To War," 8-10
     "The Cave Man," 28-30
     "Wigglers," 109-110
     "Rediscovered," 114-115
  and fear,
    see "The Attack," 44-46
    "Fear," 158-159
    use of to demoralize enemy,
     see "The Song of the
      Bayonet," 157-158
  "faint memories," 126,
    see "Through a Glass,
     Darkly," 118-122
  fighting, philosophy of, xii n16,
    68, 80, 87, 137-138, 149
    see "Absolute War," 146-147
    "The Song of the
     Bayonet," 157-158
  and fishing, 108
  on fraternization, 72
  and frontier fighters, affinity
    for, 40-41,
    see "The Forgotten Man,"
     111-113
    "The Vanished Race,"
     113
    "The Dying Race,"
     113-114
    "gentle" nature, x-xi,
     xiv, xxi
  German fear of, xvii n28, 157
  and God of Battles, 9 n19,
    see "The Attack," 44-46
    "Soldier's Religion,"
     77-78
    "God of Battles,",
     141-143
  and Goddess of War, 9 n19,
    see "To War," 8-10
  homecoming, *156*
  and honorable death,
    see "The Vision," 46-48
    "To Our First Dead,"
     80-81
    "The Moon and the
     Dead," 83-84
    "A Soldier's Burial,"
     100-101
    "Dead Pals," 101-103
    "Anti-Climax," 124-125
    "A Soldier's Prayer,"
     143 n18
  as horseman, 27
  and horses, love of, xi,
    see "Billy the Old Troop
     Horse," 15-17
    "Epitaph to a Horse," 17
    "The War Horses,"
     116-118
  and imaginative literature, xiv

173

(Patton, George, Smith Jr.)
  and immigrants, 15
  insecurities, 141
  as inspirational speaker, xx
  Italian fear of, xvi-xvii
  and Japanese, 13,
    see "The Rulers," 22-25
  and journalists, 12
  as King Arthur, 14, *132*
  and killing,
    see "The Vision," 46-48
    "Soldier's Religion,"
    77-78
    "Peace--November 11,
    1918," 84-86
  love poems,
    see Patton, Beatrice Ayer
    (wife)
  marriage, 13
  and "mask" of command, xiv,
  141
  as Master of the Sword, 48 n74
  and mathematics, 6
  medals, 87, *144*, *153*, *160*
  medievalism of, vi, xii, *132*,
    see "Oh Ye Foolish Half-
    God Mortals," 13-14
  and militia, 13 n28
  and "Mistress War,"
    see "To War," 8-10
  and mysticism,
    see "Ouija," 104-105
    "Through a Glass,
    Darkly," 118-122
    "The Soul in Battle,"
    128-129
  and Nordic mythology, xii, xvi,
    see "The Soul in Battle,"
    128-129
  as "Old Blood and Guts,"
    ix n6
  and Olympics (1912), *18*,
    126 n47
  as passé, 161
  and peace,
    see "Peace--November 11,
    1918," 84-86
  and peacetime army
    see "Servants," 12-13
  as poet, viii, xiii, xv

Patton poetry,
  anti-Memorial Day,
    see "Decoration Day,"
    122-123
    "The Lament of the
    New Heroes," 124
    "Anti-Climax," 124-125
  "bad," xxi
  critical of his own, viii, 3,
    4, 6, 36, 83, 128
  enthusiasm for his own,
    31
  eulogistic,
    see "To Our First Dead,"
    80-81
    "In Memoriam,"
    87-88
    "A Soldier's Burial,"
    100-101
  historical,
    see "Out of Hell," 126-128
  ironic,
    see "The Fly," 38-40
    "Mud," 53-55
    "The Song of the
    Embusqué," 58-59
    "Progress," 105-106
    "Majority Law," 107
    "Oh, Little Town of
    Houffalize," 155
  love,
    see Patton, Beatrice Ayer
    (wife)
  meditative,
    see "The Pacific," 131
  publication of, viii, xv, 28,
    30, 157, 159
  role of in Patton's life, viii, xiii,
    xvi, 4, 19, 47, 57, 59, 85,
    123, 129
  sado-comic,
    see "The Fly," 38-40
    "Mud," 53-55
    "Mercenary's Song
    (A.D. 1600)," 75-77
    "Forgotten Dwellings,"
    129-130
  satirical,
    see "The Slacker," 71-72
    "You Never Can Tell
    About a Woman," 73

(Patton, George, Smith Jr.)
  "Recollections--A.E.F.,"
    74-75
  "Mercenary's Song,"
    75-77
  "The Yellow Legs,"
    92-94
  "That Must Be Benson,"
    137-139
  "Seven-Up!" 143-146
  "Absolute War," 146-147
  "The Life and Death of
    Colonel Gasenoyl,"
    147-153
  "Reference," 154-155
  scatological,
    see "The Fly," 38-40
    "The Turds of the
      Scouts," 40-42
    "The Song of the Turds
      of Langres," 69-70
  sensuous,
    see "The Rape of the
      Carribean," 130
  spontaneous,
    see "Decoration Day,"
      122-123
    "The Lament of the
      New Heroes," 124
    "Anti-Climax," 124-125
  written for him, xiv
  political aspirations, 23 n41
  and politicians, 12, 19, 80
    see "The Rulers," 22-25
    "To Wilson," 30-32
  and popular music, vi
  as "pot bound" soldier, 12, 137
  and public relations, 137
  and psychological warfare,
    see "The Song of the
      Bayonet," 157-158
  as "Quill Georgie," 71 n38
  reading (WWII), ix n5
  reconciliation of "warrior"
    nature and "gentle" soul, x
  and reincarnation, xv, 14,
    see "Memories Roused by a
      Roman Theater," 65
    "The Vanished Race,"
      113
    "Rediscovered," 114-115
    "Through a Glass,
      Darkly," 118-122
    "The Sword of
      Lono," 133-134
  on "rough" talk, 69-70
  sense of humor, xiv
  sentimentality, xi n11, 15, 17
  as singer, *140*
  and slapping incidents, x,
    145-146 n20
  and social Darwinism, xii
  "soft side," xi n11, xiv
  as soldier's god,
    see "God of Battles,"
      141-143
  and sports, 6, 112, 126,
    see "Florida," 108-109
  as swordsman, 48 n74, *27*
  and tank warfare, 61, 65, *67*,
    see "The Precious Babies,"
      68-69
  "Regret," 81-82
  "Bill," 88-90
  urination in Rhine, 161
  and veterans, 12 n25,
    see "Decoration Day,"
      122-123
    "The Lament of the
      New Heroes," 124
    "Anti-Climax," 124-125
  and warrior spirit, x, xxi, 19,
    84,
    see "The Forgotten Man,"
      111-113
    "The Vanished Race,"
      113
    "The Dying Race,"
      113-114
    "Through a Glass,
      Darkly," 118-122
    "The Soul in Battle,"
      128-129
    "God of Battles,"
      141-143
    "Duty," 161-162
  As West Point cadet, *xxiv*
  wounded, 84
  as writer of imaginative
    literature, xiv
Patton Museum of Cavalry and
  Armor, Ft. Knox, KY, xviii

Patton, Ruth Ellen (daughter), v, 60, 76, 126
Pershing, John J., 19, 28, 47, 53, 73, 92, 94 n83
psychagogia, xvii

Q

Queckmeyer, John G., 54, 59

R

Reagan, Ronald, xviii
Rommel, Erwin, 138
Roosevelt, Franklin D., xi, xx, 158
Roosevelt, Theodore, and "strenuous life," xii
Rubio Ranch shootout, 19, 41, 47, 116
Russians, 150

S

St. Mihiel Offensive (WWI), 19, 84, 89 n69, 99
Schofield Barracks, HI, 130
Scott, George C., xix n33, 118
Scott, Sir Walter, vi, 25
2nd Armored Division, xv, 137
Semmes, Harry, 149-150
Service, Robert W., vi, 26
Seventh Army,
  see "Seven Up!" 143-146
Shakespeare, William, vi;
  As You Like It, 4 n5, 7 n13;
  Henry V, 7 n13, see also,
  "God of Battles," 141-143;
  Macbeth, 7 n14;
  "Sonnet 18," 7
Sicily, invasion of, 143
social Darwinism, xii,
  see "The Cave Man," 28-30
Southey, Robert, 25
Stimson, Henry L., xi-xii
Swinburne, Algernon Charles, 25

T

Taft, William Howard, xi
tanks (WWI), *50*, *67*, *91*, 92
  ancient forerunners of 65 n24
  infancy of, 61, 65
  6.5-ton light Renault ("Baby Tank"), *67*, 68
    see "The Precious Babies," 68-69
  "Regret," 81-82
  "Bill," 88-90
Tate, 70
Tennyson, Alfred, Lord, vi;
  Ulysses, 103;
  "The Revenge: A Ballad of the Fleet," 126
Third Army, viii, *136*, 145, 146 161-162
304th American Tank Brigade, *50*, 89 n69
Thomson, James, "The City of Dreadful Night,"
  see "The City of Dreadful Light," 115-116
Time (cover), *136*
Turner, Robert A., xx-xxi n39

V

Villa, Pancho, 19, 40, 93 n81
Virginia Military Institute, v, xix n33, 3, 6

W

Wainwright, Jonathan M., 4
Wallace, Mike, xviii
War,
  as "beautiful intellectual contest," 33
  as "biological necessity," xii
  as "business," 80 n51
  divine significance of, xii
  ennobling nature of, xiii
  "joy of," xi

"joyous privilege" of dying in battle,
   see "To Our First Dead," 80-81
  as "magnificent competition," xiii, 143
  as "moral necessity," xii
  Patton's "strange" attraction to, 12
  as prerequisite to civilization, xii
    see "To War," 8-10
      "Servants," 12-13
      "The Attack," 44-46
      "The End of War,"
      "Through a Glass, D Darkly," 118-122
West Point (U.S. Military Academy),
  ix n6, xx-xxi n39, 3, 11, 12, 71 n38,
  see "The Five Stages of Cadet Life," 4-5
    "The Life of a Cadet," 6-7
  see also The Howitzer
Wilson, Woodrow, 19, 32, 47
    "too proud to fight" speech, 21,
  see "To Wilson," 30-32
Woman's Home Companion,
  see frontispiece,
    "God of Battles," 141-143
Wood, Leonard, xi-xii
World War I, xiii, 21, 22, 30, 47, *50, 51-94, 67, 79, 91*
  end of,
    see "Peace-November 11, 1918," 84-86
  use of animals in,
    see "The War Horses," 116-118
World War II, *frontispiece*, ix, 61, 133, 135-162, *136, 140, 144, 148, 153, 156, 160*
  Patton as decoy in, 157
  Patton sidelined during, 145

STUDIES IN AMERICAN LITERATURE

1. Robert Molloy, **The Letters (1971-1977) of Robert Molloy**, Melvin B. Yoken (ed.)
2. Elizabeth I. Hanson, **The American Indian in American Literature: A Study in Metaphor**
3. Cliff Lewis and Carroll Britch (eds.), **Rediscovering Steinbeck-Revisionist Views of His Art, Politics, and Intellect**
4. Elizabeth I. Hanson, **Thoreau's Indian of the Mind**
5. A. Carl Bredahl and Susan Lynn Drake, **Hemingway's *Green Hills of Africa* as Evolutionary Narrative: Helix and Scimitar**
6. Thomas Maik, **Mark Twain's *Joan of Arc* and the Heroine as Divine Child**
7. Robert Deamer, **The Importance of Place in the American Literature of Hawthorne, Thoreau, Crane, Adams, and Faulkner: American Writers, American Culture, and the American Dream**
8. George S. Patton, Jr., **The Poems of General George S. Patton, Jr.**, Carmine A. Prioli (ed.)
9. Melinda M. Ponder, **Hawthorne's Early Narrative Art**
10. Jessica Haigney, **Walt Whitman and the French Impressionists: A Study of Analogies**
11. Mary R. Ryder, **Willa Cather and the Classical Myth: The Search for a New Parnassus**